The 365 Days of Happiness bestselling author

JACQUELINE PIRTLE

Parenting
through
the
Eyes
of
Lollipops

D0873424

ISBN-13: 978-1-7320851-2-1

Published by: FreakyHealer

Editor-in-chief: Zoe Pirtle

Editor/layout: Mitch Pirtle

Book cover design by Kingwood Creations
kingwoodcreations.com

Author photo courtesy of Lionel Madiou
madiouART.com

Hair Styling by Alejandro Jimenez
@alejandrojimenezofficial (IG)

ACKNOWLEDGMENTS

The most incredible creations happen when a beautiful team pulls together! Thank you for your dedication to make this book tangible. I give my appreciation to Zoe Mina Pirtle for her editorial mastery; Mitch Pirtle for his editorial and layout love; kingwoodcreations.com for their fun and polished book cover design; madiouART.com for an amazing photo shoot; and @alejandrojimenezofficial (IG) for his masterful hair design.

I also would like to give a huge "Thank You!" to everyone and everything who urged me to write the next book, to all who are always supporting me, and to Kelsey Butts of BookPublicityServices for her impeccable promotion of *365 Days of Happiness* and ***Parenting Through the Eyes Of Lollipops***.

And last but not least, thanks to all the lollipops out there—I love you to no end.

DEDICATION

I dedicate this book to my wonderfully phenomenal children;
Zoe Pirtle and Till Pirtle, and our sweet cats… Your invitation
for me to BE your mom made this book possible—your training,
your support, your inspirations, your infinite love, your laughter,
and your smiles are all part of these teachings that will help
children all around the world to live happy lives.

Thank you! I love you to the moon and back, and more, and
most… ~ Your Mom

A WORD BY THE AUTHOR

I hope you enjoy this book as much as I loved writing it. If you do, it would be wonderful if you could take a short minute and leave a review on Amazon.com and Goodreads.com as soon as you can, as your kind feedback is much appreciated and so very important. Thank you.

I also want to let you know that there is the *365 Days of Happiness* book - which supports the teachings in *Parenting Through the Eyes of Lollipops* - that I have written. *365 Days of Happiness* is available in paperback, kindle, a companion mobile application for both Android and iPhone, and can be supplemented with the appropriate self-study program that you can find at www.freakyhealer.com.

CONTENTS

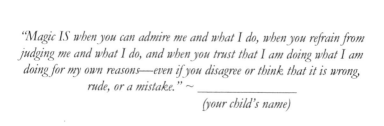

"Magic IS when you can admire me and what I do, when you refrain from judging me and what I do, and when you trust that I am doing what I am doing for my own reasons—even if you disagree or think that it is wrong, rude, or a mistake." ~ _____

(your child's name)

HI, I AM THE AUTHOR!

My name is Jacqueline Pirtle. I pride myself deeply and consciously in being fully in love with the most truth-finding job there is; being a mom, a parent—a privilege in every sense.

To top my parenting experience off with a heap of sweetness, I get to share my life and happiness with my wonderful husband of over 23 years.

I was given the honor to claim my mom throne by two amazing young-adult humans who are thriving and living their truths, going for what they love, and are an inspiration through and through. I am also a chosen mom to many furry ones—some of whom have transitioned back to non-physical by now and will never be forgotten but always cherished.

I wrote this book because clearly it wanted to be written—it found me to be written, and I am glad that I listened! Hence, the reason why everything around me was about "babies and children"—in perfect synchronicity with being focused and in alignment with my soul calling.

One graceful energy in particular was a great inspiration with its presence as a butterfly, blessing me by making my head its runway to play on and hanging out on the hammock next to me while writing this book in my back yard. When I asked, "Who are you?" I sensed and knew that it was the energetic essence of our third beautiful baby who transitioned way before even taking a first breath of air, because its soul experience was complete. Pure graciousness in every way!

Not to mention the baby bunny that suddenly was in our yard every time I sat down to write, the baby cardinal bird that learned how to fly in front of my eyes, and the mommy blue-jay that shrieked at me from the top of her lungs because the feeders were empty—her kids needed food.

Besides all that family love and joy, there is also an infinite amount of magic in my work as a holistic practitioner, a healing arts teacher and mentor, and author of the bestseller *365 Days of Happiness*. My unique passion as an ambassador for mindful happiness shines through in all of my life, my work, and me.

The inspiration and the words for this book flowed through me in ease and playfulness, just as the words for *365 Days of Happiness* did. I know with certainty that these words are right for me to write because when I open that floodgate and start typing, I feel cleansed, healthy, happy, refreshed, and vivid. The energy that is moving through me puts a smile on my face and makes me a happy mom—spreading infinite goodness to everyone and everything around me, my children, husband, pets, and beyond.

If I would hold any of this back, I would get all sorts of *verklempt*—energetically gunked-up.

I invite you, Mom and Dad, to join me and open up your inspirational floodgates too. Start doing - full time or part time - what creates your happy juices, shifting yourself to BE and live in a happy frequency—spreading and sharing that with your children, spouses, and pets.

That is a great first step towards **Parenting Through the Eyes of Lollipops!**

Of course I did have my fair share of ups and downs and lefts and rights as a mom, however after trying to blame my kids at first - which never worked and only created a huge well of more unwell feelings - I learned to always look at myself first, and to take full responsibility of all that is in my life for me. Makes sense since it is fact that I create my life, that I am in charge of all that IS, and that I have full control of my thoughts and how I feel about anything and anyone—including about how my children or how the world behaves.

I truly wrote both, this book and *365 Days of Happiness*, from my heart, my inner knowing, my soul being, and through being deeply connected with the universe, the quantum field, physical life, and the highest essence of the divine—a space where everything IS possible, BE-able, and live-able.

One more thing that I do want to brag about - bragging is one of the most phenomenal mood enhancers I learned to do while being a parent - is that I attended the best university there IS to study deeply, and in detail, the art of **Parenting Through the Eyes of Lollipops**.

The "Pirtle Kids University"—THE best parenting school there is! For me, at least.

By studying parenting intensely through being a mom and - still to this day - by being open to continuously learning from and through my children, I am always in the stage of becoming the best version of being me and the best version of being a parent—in my eyes, the juiciest life experience ever!

So thank you "Pirtle Kids University" for choosing me and for having me!

My intentions for this book are that:

- When you are simply just holding this book, it feels like you are holding your child's sacred inner being - its soul, its heart, and its inner knowing - in your gracious hands

- When you are hugging it, you ARE hugging your child's higher self and wellbeing

- When you are reading these words they bring a clear understanding of your child's presence and essence in your life, and shift you deeply inside of your own heart and soul

- This book represents the love between you and your child

Furthermore, by reading and practicing this book, your deep love, gratitude, and appreciation for your child IS being initiated, sparked, re-found, and nourished, and is growing into infinite magnificence—creating magic that you get to enjoy with your children. They will be forever thankful, believe me!

Take from this book what fits for you and leave the rest be, because you and only you know what's best for you and your family—that is always so! No exceptions ever!

What is the biggest takeaway from being a parent?

Never look at the children for betterment or ask them to change so you can feel better. Instead, focus on yourself, take full responsibility of how you feel, and own what is happening in your life—setting your children free so they can BE themselves.

All of the teachings in this book play a vital role for me and are flowing in the essence of magic into my life as a mom, wife, woman, and whole being—my body, mind, soul, and my consciousness.

I recommend for you to catch on to this love of being a parent and to take this magic by the hand, so that you and your children can enjoy the high-for-life experience of being together and dancing the harmonious dance that binds you forever.

Yours truly,

Jacqueline

All of the contents are my personal views and opinions. They do not replace medical or psychological help, and never support or advocate abuse in any way. Get yourself and your children all the help that is needed—your children deserve only the best and so do you.

INTRODUCTION

This book is about lighting or re-lighting your light in you as a mom or dad. It's about starting or re-starting your experience with your child, a precious soul who chose to make this transition into physical life—with you as the parent(s).

Mom, you are this precious soul's host when you are expecting—besides being half the power to make it happen. You signed up to give physical birth to this non-physical energetic being, who is here to experience physical life. Your heart is urging you to explode with the love that is expanding in you through this magnificent physical life experience.

Dad, no worries, you are of infinite importance too—through being the other half of the make-it-happen power and your own unique dad love-feelings that are emerging you have the power to bring limitless strength to the occasion, for both the mom and child to nourish from.

"I am here to help you shift yourself closest to your own soul being—to become one and whole as you."

~ Your Child

When you choose, when you wish for, or when you desire to have a child, you are not - and never are - giving yourself or anything up. That is an easy thought and feeling to have, since you are hopefully all wrapped up in beautiful excitement for the child to arrive. Drench yourself in that well-feeling frequency fully and completely by consciously feeling over the moon. From there, know that you can feel even better!

Yes! You can feel even higher by building on top of that exhilarating feeling - it's like building a tower on top of an already incredible high building - through consciously focusing on being excited that you are becoming more, that you are expanding, and that you will be a better you because of being a parent—

regardless of whether the child is already here or about to make an appearance. That is what parenting does for you.

When you are not choosing to have a child, yet still are having a child, it is the same! You are not giving yourself or anything up —ever! You are becoming more by either choosing to have that child or through choosing not to have that child. Let this sink in for a minute: "You are becoming more!" no matter the why, the how, the what, or the fitting solution.

You are becoming more!

It is of utmost importance to understand, and to agree on, that being a mom and dad does not mean you own your children; nor are you really ever in charge of your child.

Let me explain:

- We live in a vibrational energetic universe

- Everything is energy—energy is all there is

- We exchange and share our energies with each other at all times

- Everyone as a whole being, is a physical body, a mind, a soul, and a consciousness

- Everyone is part physical and part non-physical

- The non-physical - the soul - is the bigger part and is our eternal guidance system

- We are all here in this physical space as one and the same— energetic soul beings who are experiencing physical life by being in our physical bodies

- The reason that everyone is physically here - in these physical bodies and on this physical earth - is to expand into who we truly are by experiencing and learning about humanity

- We all create our own experiences in this physical life

Meaning…

The only two differences between parents and children are that the former give physical life to the latter - making them a parent and the birthed one the child - and the timing of everyone's physical arrival and presence on this physical earth. That's it!

Being that we are all the same, possess the same soul guidance, and are all here for the same reason, it is obvious that nobody owns anyone—rather, everyone and everything is here to experience co-living, co-existing, co-creating, co-experiencing, and co-expanding.

To get deeper into the teachings of energy, vibrations, frequencies, quantum physics, law of attraction, and what the universe is made of, contact me at FreakyHealer.com or search for a teacher that fits your style.

No-one is less and no-one is more! Ever!

I based this book and my teachings on three rock-solid, practiced, and proven-to-no-end pillars. They nourish the experience of gracious parenthood and all there is to know about **Parenting Through the Eyes of Lollipops**.

The three pillars are:

1.   The Harmonious Dance

2.   It Is Never The Child

3.   The Love Cycle of Parenthood

Choosing, committing, practicing, passionately being, and freely living these teachings will ensure that you can manage, tackle, solve, nourish, enjoy, love, and enchant every situation that will pop up in this rich time with your children—making it the highest form of celebrating every soul being involved and really milking this experience of physical life to the fullest and grandest ever.

So first, let me share with you the reason behind my title—it's a bit sneaky! Then we will move into the preparation phase which will shift you to be wide open—so it is easy for you to fall in love with these three pillars. After that, you get to sit back and read about real parent-life scenarios—I call them Loose Ends.

I urge you to be patient and read slowly from front to back - even if you are desperate to find out how to handle explosions that are staring you in the face - because giving yourself time helps you to get the hang of *Parenting Through the Eyes of Lollipops* in a way that will stick—that makes it natural for you.

So hang in there, we will get to all the juicy stuff that parenthood is made out of very soon. Promise!

PARENTING THROUGH THE EYES OF LOLLIPOPS — THE MEANING

I'm a little sneaky and I know it…

"Lollipops have this incredible power to shift us to BE and live in a frequency of magic—because that is the energy they carry and the frequency they vibrate in."

~ Jacqueline Pirtle

I chose this specific title for the book with the intention that when you read these words, you immediately shift to the right, fitting, and perfect energetic space for you to BE and live in—so that my teachings can connect with your soul being, touch your heart deeply, and so you can feel what you read.

Let's experiment…

Think of what the word "lollipop" initiates for you—playfulness, child-like, light and fun, joy, laughter, party-ish, celebration, worry-free, and colorful sweetness.

Now think of what thinking, feeling, hearing, tasting, smelling, and seeing a lollipop does for you. All of the above, but a million times more potently and vividly because it's not just the word anymore, now you also have all of your senses involved.

Try topping this feeling experiment off by licking and tasting a real lollipop and feel the well-feeling this yumminess shifts you to—incredible magic!

To explain what is happening here:

Everything is energy and always sharing its energy with everyone and everything. The lollipop shares its energetic value with you—meaning you become one with it and shift to feeling in the frequency of that lollipop.

That's why choosing such a playful title was in your best

interest and was certainly in my best interest—because I too get constantly shifted to BE and live in the perfect energy, making this book infinitely fun. It's a win, win!

Here is a "get yourself in the frequency of lollipops" meditation:

The following visualization will shift you to a state where you can choose well-feeling above all else, for yourself and for your children. Keep it handy and present, practice it with your children, and for heaven's sake go get a huge bag of lollipops—to be shared freely and used to intensify your practice of this meditation and of *Parenting Through the Eyes of Lollipops*. In other words, if trouble arises hand out lollipops and instruct everyone involved to lick the sweetness before speaking a word or taking any action.

So let's get started…

Sit comfortably in a quiet room—best would be with the doors closed. Close your eyes. Smile. Relax. Start to consciously focus on your breathing. Breathe in and imagine widening your space. Breathe out and imagine letting go of everything. Enjoy this for a little while.

When ready, imagine a huge colorful lollipop - or a whole bouquet of lollipops - of your choice. Make it well-feeling for you. Consciously look at your chosen lollipop, feel the energy it carries—one of being happy, playful, fun, light, laughing, joyous, sweet, carefree, worry-free, child-like and endless fun.

After a while, visualize walking in a circle around it—never losing sight of its sweetness. Hold that vision as long as you like. Then take a whiff, to smell your lollipop, and a lick to taste it. Such sweetness!

Sense how the magic of this lollipop shifts you to BE and live in a happy mood. You might even feel like you just travelled back in time to a playful childhood moment.

Then, start chatting with your lollipop. Say "Hello!" and ask it questions. Smile at it. Sense how creative this imaginary happening feels for you, and think of all the pleasure this lollipop has in store for you.

When ready, open your eyes and know that through this co-creation you and that lollipop are now one and the same fun energy. You have been shifted to BE and live in the well-being of your heart and soul—the home of your pure joy and happiness and a perfect place to graciously allow whatever comes your way to be.

So breathe and smile, and be assured that NOW is the perfect time to pick up the parenting job, to act on the mom and dad responsibility, and to be a presenter at the speaking engagement that is given to you by your children.

The best vibrational match to any situation is to feel good and to be happy—and the best outcome for any situation is when you are happy before you speak, hear, smell, taste, act, talk, feel, think of, and see your children.

Remember, get yourself a pack of a million lollipops ASAP!

Have them handy and never run out. Use them to either get yourself into the frequency of lollipops or watch your kids getting there, licking with enthusiasm. Then latch onto the creative energy your "lickers" create while slurping and drooling over their lollipops.

When toughness arises, pull out the lollipops and let everyone have plenty of licks before starting the discussion—who knows, after all that licking there might not even be a discussion anymore. Lollipops do that!

In gratitude and appreciation to all the lollipops out there, we love you so much!

This IS Parenting Through the Eyes of Lollipops!

LET'S TALK PREPARATION AND SET YOU UP PROPERLY

An important first step for a parent is to relax and know that you really are wonderful just by being here and by being present—ready for your new life as a parent or ready to shift into a new way as a parent. You ARE magnificent!

I invite you to say, think, and feel the following words often:

"I AM a phenomenally powerful parent with a deep inner guidance and an infinite capability to love!"

Really breathe into these words, and feel your shift to being and living in a frequency of peaceful-ness, openness, pure-ness, right-ness, and good-ness—your heart space and your soul being.

Acknowledge that you are NOT here to impress anyone, anything, or life itself—especially not your children. You are here to simply BE; nothing else. Feel the release of all resistance and the pressure-free space that you create for yourself by acknowledging this.

So what does to BE or not to BE really mean?

Do you think to BE means you have to have hard times and BE miserable? I surely hope not, because to BE clearly means to feel well, to be happy, to enjoy, and to feel excited about your existence and expansion. Just think about how well you feel by reading the first few paragraphs about your magnificence, and how wonderful it feels to acknowledge that all you have to do is BE your soul being which is pure positive energy.

Now shift your focus to your children. Let them - born or unborn - know that they too are wonderful and magnificent just as they ARE. Fill them in, that coming into this physical life means they are here to BE themselves—nothing else. Let your child know of this magic and well-feeling through loving and uplifting words, thoughts - every thought is energy that is shared - actions, happenings, and, for older children, through explanation and education.

Make well-feeling a priority for you because it spreads to your children, filling every single cell of their whole being - body, mind, soul, consciousness - with goodness, and it returns that high-for-life energy to you like a boomerang.

Think about the incredible power that is used to lift a sinking ship to be afloat again—you feeling wonderful is that power that can lift any child to be emotionally afloat again.

Feeling wonderful IS powerful!

Knowing that the entwinement between parents and children is such a powerful love-wonder and deeply sacred time - that is experienced on both the physical and non-physical level - it is only normal that no one should ever feel bad, unworthy, wrong, or less than the other in this wholeness of being. Rather, only feel the deepest of love and understanding for each other—no matter the circumstances.

You give them physical life and they give you the life and soul experience of parenthood. Think about this phenomenal exchange that is possible when consciously lived. Realize how much more and how much bigger you both will get by really opening up to this expansion, and by dancing in harmony.

With you taking the lead - because that is what you signed up for - to shift to a gracious way of parenting, you are letting yourself dance freely with your child—serving both your soul being and their soul being without limits or rules and without thoughts of ownership, without one owing the other, and without wanting anything in return, making this the purest exchange ever.

So make a pact with yourself, and celebrate the grandest love there is in its full royal-ness by initiating and nourishing it with gratitude and appreciation for the value of a lifetime. Meditate on this beautiful love—as one and in full! Then practice this reflection often throughout your parenthood journey—especially when you feel anything less than love for your child, when you don't feel a connection with them, or when you don't understand your children.

Nobody owns anyone!

To be on phenomenal terms with your child means you acknowledge that your child is a soul being, outfitted with a soul guidance and a soul calling. You can leave your child to BE as IS - as its soul being IS - because on a soul level no soul ever asks the other soul to be different. That is only an in-physical-life occurrence. That way, you child can do exactly what it is supposed to do—BE.

But there is more…

You also want to have your own phenomenal life experience of being a parent and you want to feel really good by having it all —the appetizer, entree, dessert, and the espresso at the end.

Feeling really good about being a parent and the "bigger and more" of what you are becoming is only possible if you play by the energetic rules: that we are all the same, that we are all souls, and that we all want to experience physical life on our own terms.

Some might say, "but I had a rough childhood, bad things happened, I was not loved, and I was never shown…"

That does not matter!

You are being a parent to a not-yet-born or an already born younger or older child—that is a brand new experience. Talking about an old story, and letting that not-true-anymore tale, bleed into the new magic that is ready for you and your child to experience is like tainting a new fresh dessert with the cream from yesterday—yuck!

You know better and different now; you have expanded and are more and bigger, and your heart says differently on how to deal with or feel a situation—one in which you are now the parent to your own child.

So don't revive your old stories to be the focus point of your NOW! The old was what it was, and helped create the amazing you that you are now. Let it all go like old dirt blows off a car when driven forward with speed—heck, leave a nice big black tire mark by saying, "Enough, I am going full speed into what's new." End of story.

Write that new story! Keep it fresh, fun, and as you want it to feel for you and your children—by following your soul guidance to be a happy parent who enjoys spending happy times with happy children.

Every split second IS new!

Separate yourself from being your children, because you are not your children!

Feel for your children but don't BE and live them, and don't take over the feelings that they feel—you are not them and they are not you. You two are separate soul beings; both here to BE a non-physical energy in a physical body—experiencing physical life to expand into your own ways. And through that separateness, you are one with your children.

Feeling, being, and living your child's feelings fully and vividly spreads your strong feelings - that are a mix of new and old resurfaced ones - as an energy-cocktail to your child, filling every cell of their being with energy that is not even theirs.

If it is positive energy, it can be a wonderful filler for your child. However, if it is of a negative nature, then it is a very hefty filler, making them feel heavy, which can show up as emotional distress. Imagine the mess that this creates!

I say, keep your energy squeaky clean by not being your child, instead seeing your child as whole, powerful, and capable, and as their own soul being guiding them to always know what is best for them—of course with the exception of danger. For instance, when crossing the street in unsafe ways; that is when you take over and help them without budging.

If there is no danger, then trust!

Trust that they got it! Because they do. They understand; they want to do well, they are good people; they are wise soul-beings, and they are pure positive energy.

Free kids thrive, because free souls thrive; creatively, intellectually, in aliveness, and in physical life form—in body, mind, soul, and consciousness.

Understanding this creates a peacefully beautiful space that is full of clarity—for how you want to enjoy this sacred parent-child experience, about what kind of parent you want to BE and expand into, and what you and your children are here to do.

So get the popcorn out, sit comfortably, relax, and watch them BE—without noise, words, or comments. Breathe, but that is all you really should do, to not interrupt them in their being or interfere with who they really are.

A free being thrives!

When co-creating with children, it is crucial for you to understand that you are infusing them and yourself with a love that you had no idea was even possible or is existing in you, for you, or in life—period.

Parenthood is, most of the time, the best arrangement that you have ever experienced—but sometimes also the hardest that you have ever mastered. For the hard times, and to get off the blame game immediately, this is not and never was a "Who's fault is it?" situation. Fault never needs to have space during hard times with your children.

Here is why…

Parenting can be hard at times, just as life can be hard at

times, because in these times you are shown how much of a faulty old-recording-state you are living and feeling—how untrue, unfitting, and unwell-feeling your old beliefs and thought patterns are for you.

Hard times - or better said, when you think, see, and feel them as hard - are a clear indication of how far away from your soul calling you are, and offer you the gift of getting back on track with your expansion into who you really are. They are a chance to correct your direction from unhappy to happy—turning hard times into nothing other than a compass of your soul. I invite you to rejoice and celebrate those times with a warm welcome.

Embrace the compass of your soul!

Here are some creative save-the-day ideas for you to shift yourself and your children to BE and live in the frequency harmony:

Imagination at its best. Imagine a horse called Enjoyment! Tell your kids to hop on and hold tight—ride it into the sunset with them! Catch on to the sparkles in their eyes, then sparkle up yourself, and feel how your time with your children becomes vividly magical. Imagination with your children changes everything, and besides, they are masters of the imagination!

Speak to everything—not everyone. Let's say a bird grabs your attention. Stop and really see, hear, and feel that bird. Start to chat with it—speak to that bird. Say "Hello!" and thank the bird for its presence. Ask the bird about its well being. You might even want to ask what wisdom the bird has in store for you—what is it mirroring you? Is it its freedom, the wingspan of what it can cover, or is it its beauty? Whatever it is telling you is exactly what you need to hear and experience right now.

Invite your children to chat with everything around them too—in truth, they probably think that you are a slow-poke since you only just realized that you can talk to everything.

- Talk to your food!

- Talk to the air!

- Talk to the sun, moon, and sky!

- Talk to the rain!

- Talk to your shoes!

Make chatting with everything out loud a common practice with your children. Not only is this loads of fun, you also are playing with the universal law that everything is energy, the same energy, and sharing its energies at all times—and that all energy carries information and knowledge for whoever is inclined to listen.

Keep your child's talkative mood alive by allowing and nourishing it early on, and if your child is older, start showing that you - the mighty parent! - are chatting with everything that grabs your attention.

Your environment has so much to give to you—open wide and allow this expansion of experiences to fill you and your children in every new split second of your life.

Keep the goofy-ness going. Craft, be creative, play, imagine, pretend, and enrich your child's goofy-ness by letting yourself become an enchanted goofball. I highly recommend you to not hold back, but to be of infinite fun with your children, actually, let them take the reins of leadership in the goofy department— they are much better at it than you, with your old and already worn goof-tracks.

Here is a personal example…

When my children were young, every time someone spilled something it was a frustrated situation. One day I thought, "There has to be a better way." From that day on I said, "Wonderful, your spill just fed the fairies! They are lucky that you feed them so well." Can you imagine the shocked eyes I got, the first time I said that? It was wonderful. From then on, spills were very goofy happenings—at least most of the time. It made us happy that the fairies got fed. And anyways, whoever came up with the thought that fairies don't exist, let alone are not "hangry," or are not waiting to be fed?

When children are inspired... When children have ideas - even when they are eyebrow lifting for you - let them have these inspirations and help fulfill them. If dangerous, get in the way, but not by saying "no." Instead, find a solution to make the idea safe so that they can still experience the important idea they had.

Kids are infinitely creative! They grab the force of their deep inner self-knowing and come up with incredibly original ideas. If allowed, they are inspiring and worth expanding into, so it's better to consider joining them in their creativity versus following the option of not joining them, because a "no" shuts down the idea and their inner self—slowly quieting their inner force and voice to the point where they can't hear it anymore, or forcing it louder than ever.

They become either "good kids," behaving always nicely and politely - a pleaser child - or a rebel who constantly fights you. In both scenarios, it's because their soul being is undermined.

And just for thought, later in their lives we tell them to follow their gut and their heart, asking them to grow and strengthen what got shot down in the first place—and some end up going through therapy for that.

For more fun exercises, actually 365 of them, pick up a copy of my bestselling book *365 Days of Happiness*!

Every experience that a child wants, chooses, or creates has the potential to be a healing opportunity for you. Maybe it is something that you never got to do - filling your emptiness by doing it now - or it might be that you had a bad experience in the past, which you get to override with a good one this time. Not to mention all the wonderful memories you create by joining them in what they want, and the magic you get to witness because what they want is always for the same reason—to feel good.

As an example:

Imagine your child wants to paint right now, at night, and inside. You say "no," because it's late and the mess is too big for indoors—you can already see it.

Your child's idea is born from a creative inspiration and inner calling of their soul. Whereas your "no" reasons originate from your old beliefs and recordings of "it's too late," and "painting is messy, it should be practiced either outside, in a specific painting room, or in art class," or "I am too tired for this," "I have so much to do tomorrow…"

If your "no" originates from being exhausted, realize that your physical exhaustion is a dis-alignment between who you are in physical life and who you really are energetically and soul-fully. Following your soul calling always comes from an energizing place because you are following your never exhausting truth, while following a physical calling that is not in sync with your soul is a constant upstream motion—very exhausting.

Saying "no" robs your child of living, experiencing, growing, and deepening the creativity that is inspired by the soul being. You also rob yourself of an expansion that this experience has in store for you, which could be very healing and revealing for you.

Saying "Yes!" to your child's soul-calling by letting your child paint - inside, at night, and right now - is a vital and vivid creativity-shot into the veins of your soul-life and your child's soul being.

I invite you to say "YES!" and be creative with your child as often as possible, to fill yourself to the brim with the energy of creation, and to allow the magnificent shift from the old unfitting into new and exciting. My added hope here is that by saying "yes" your exhaustion has left the barn. If that's not the case take a pillow and nap beside your creative child—energizing yourself by just being there, because energy spreads.

There are millions of opportunities in every hour for you to co-create magic with your child. All YOU have to do is say "yes" more often, and stay out of your child's soul-way—watch, learn, and be a part of that guaranteed enchantment with openness and excitement.

You might think that this means you are giving in, but that is not so! Increasing your willingness to be a freer parent to your free children increases your happiness in being and living a free parenthood.

And just for thought, is it really so bad to "give in" to something so true, so pure, and so gracious, like your child's soul being? Is it really so hard to "give in" to BE and live happy, free, successfully, loved, abundantly, healthy, and vividly with your children?

I say, let go of all those reins and let the joy-horse carry you and your children freely and wildly into the sunset with infinite pleasure, the loudest laughter ever, and a ton of in-awe-ness!

Oh, and by the way…

Have you had ice cream with your children today? No? What, it's too late?

NEVER is it too late for any kind of fun! Get right at it, go get your children or wake them—fill those ice cream bowls to the brim, say "mmmmm…" with every spoon that goes in. Giggle the whole way, and feel and see what happens for you and your children.

Instead of "no" choose "yes!"

Parenting is a truth seeking mission. Sometimes you might not seek the truth or rather, you don't want to face the truth, and that's okay—but there is really no other way than to give in and look. If needed, grab your head and turn it in the direction of the truth—you might even want to consider staring at it for a while.

Shock, anger, frustration, sadness, tears, and even denial can be felt at first. Hey, you might even want to run in the opposite direction. However, when you come to realize the incredible learning, healing, and expansion that is presented to you through this truth, you will want to consciously choose to become a truth seeker and truth lover—especially when that truth is offered by your children. They love you!

And seriously, no one has ever said "I want to stay the same forever!" Here is your chance to keep evolving.

Some say that the truth hurts. That is only the case if you choose to be hurt by it—meaning, you are so disconnected with who you really are and are so out-of-love with yourself that judging yourself or others wins the case.

If you decide that the truth is your expansion and your way to get to know yourself intimately, any truth will set you free to BE and live happily in your experience of parenthood—or at least happily, until the next truth is revealed to you by your ever-so-helpful and diligent children. Then you must choose again—to look and to set yourself free as can be.

I have always been a truth seeker, and found that as long as I look through the eyes of my soul my truth looks sweet and colorful—and lollipop-ish.

Enjoy your truth and the wisdom it has in store for you. You are in for the sweetest of treats—you get to BE and live as the best and most expanded you there IS.

One more thing…

Sometimes the temptation to believe that your truth is your child's truth - meaning the disagreement is not yours but your child's doing - can be very strong. Don't let yourself be fooled! Your feelings are always your feelings. Your child is simply the messenger - the mirror - doing exactly what it promised to do when coming into your life—showing you your truth.

I am over the moon excited to drop-ship to you that your

child is ready to dance wildly and vividly with you—that IS what they came forth to do.

So let the revealing truth-party begin by giving your child the speaker podium in the next chapter!

This IS Parenting Through the Eyes of Lollipops!

HI MOM! HI DAD!

Peekaboo, it's your precious child!

I am jumping-for-joy happy, that you are willing to read what our time together really is all about—what this "you and I" is all about, and how we can experience the best time together.

I want to make your life and your time as a parent easier and more enjoyable—I want that for you and of course, I want that very much for me too. How will I make your life easier? Well, not necessarily through my "doing" but by letting you off the hook.

You might not think right now - especially if I am still a tiny baby - that it will be hard being my parent. But trust me, at some point it will be, because I personally will make sure that's the case —after all, it is part of my job being your child. Don't worry, I'll be gentle, or at least that is how I intend it to be.

Until then, think of me as a beam of light shining straight into your beam of light; my heart loving straight into your heart; and my soul smiling directly into your soul. I really, really, really love you!

Now that I have spilled my heart out, let's get you off the hook.

I wish for you to have a light - instead of heavy - time being my parent. Think of "light" as playful, joyous, and being light-hearted—not taking every single thing involving me so seriously. Even though I love being the center of your attention, it puts pressure on you and on me.

I want you to go easy on yourself, therefore going easy on me —versus being hard on yourself and being hard on me. We both deserve this precious experience of being alive together to be the happiest and most magical time ever. Don't you agree?

And…

I want you to make space for me! Yes, I need lots of space to BE and live as me in your life. So stop occupying yourself with all the unwell-feeling about everyone and everything - especially me - because that unwell-feeling does not leave me space to just be with you.

I AM very excited for this "you and I!"

When things happen, they happen for a reason. I am no coincidence! Me coming into your life happened for a reason and in our journey together there will always be new reasons—because we constantly change. Clearly this means that we will never stop finding new reasons and never will run out of reasons for why we are meant for each other. It is the most beautiful reason-journey ever—us together.

Here is a list of some of my reasons:

- I want to unleash the most powerful love in you. A love so strong, you never even thought and knew IS possible for you to feel. That IS my first reason to be here with you—if I am already born, mission accomplished. This love will show itself to you as the biggest power you will ever possess - just think of testing a mama bear - available whenever you wish to use it, feel it, and share it. You are welcome! I love you so very much!

- I want to completely turn your life upside down and awaken new and grand experiences, feelings, thoughts, senses, loves, strengths, and hardships in you and for you. Ultimately they are all already in you—ready to rise, to be lived, experienced, and/or to be healed fully and vividly by you!

Not to mention that I make your life:

- Richer—not always in money. Sorry!

- Harder—it's a good thing. Promise!

- Easier—just think of when you get to use my existence or my tantrum to get out of a gathering.

- Busier—what would you do without me? You could be bored.

- More meaningful—you loving me IS one of the most beautiful meanings of life. EVER!

Your main reason to be here as my parent is to create the opportunity for me to be alive in this physical world and to give birth to me. If I am already born, thank you! I love you so, so, so much!

Naturally, and from a physical life's point of view, you think of me coming into this word as this cute, small, and somewhat helpless little baby who is new to this earth and needs your help and attention. And in truth, I am pretty cute.

However, that thinking of "I desperately need your help, support, and guidance or else…" is only true on the physical life level. From a non-physical viewpoint, what I really am is the same as you—a non-physical soul being who is here to experience this physical life and expand into my true being.

To explain…

I chose to come here to BE with you! I chose you! How else do you think I came to BE with the perfect mom and dad?

I chose to come into this physical life to experience my own physical journey - not yours - while unleashing and enjoying a new love in you and in me, for you and for me.

I am here to love you just the way you are, even if I voice the opposite or my actions don't always look or feel as such. Fact is, me thinking that you are not cool AS IS, is on me, not on you. The invitation for you in that situation is to stay deeply grounded in being you. Please do, as I will hardly be satisfied anyways in that phase of my physical life. The phase will pass, I promise, it actually passes speedier when you stand your ground by staying who you are—without taking things too personally or noticing my un-kind feelings too much. To recap, don't ever change for me or become different because you are my parent, instead, let all your changes be for your own reasons. Consider yourself kindly warned!

I chose to come and help you as your feeling barometer. My actions initiate feelings that were already in you, showing that what you feel because of me, is always about you. I am just your server—so feel them plentifully and heal them beautifully. For example: If you are angry at me, I just served you your un-happiness. If you are laughing with me, I just served you your happiness. You are here in this physical life to BE and live your own soul being fully and completely—my mirroring is my gift to do just that.

And truthfully, I chose to come so I could be helped by you. Yes, I want your help—remember that when I am stubborn or a teenager giving no clear signals for you to help me. Find a way to do so anyways; gently and fittingly for my soul being to thrive.

You don't own me and I don't own you, and I don't always live your way and you don't always live my way. It is supposed to be like that. I want to be able to freely and fully become a more, bigger, and expanded me—I am here for me. Sure, through you, but for me. I have things to say, happenings to experience, feelings to feel, and a whole life to live as me. That is why I yearn to only be me and not a mix of you and I.

If you wonder how I will learn to behave or be a good person - with giving me complete freedom - well, I AM already all that goodness that you want me to be—no need to grow any grey hairs over how to teach me. I already AM all of that!

Fact is, we each have our separate reasons and journeys and need to be respectful of that. That lets me stay who I AM and become more of what I AM—and believe me, I am one cool baby, child, young adult, and adult, whom you get to call your child. So fluster with pride!

If this makes you think that you are getting the short end of the stick here, know that's not true. I am here to mirror you how to be your truest soul being by reflecting everything that is going on in you, back to you. I am here to grow you, show you, teach you, enlighten you, love you, mirror you, and bring you to a new level of life with this experience called "parenting."

You are very welcome!

Know that I got this, and without too many limitations I am able to do new things in new ways, find new solutions, and expand in fresh ways—and might actually present something new to others in this new-ness.

As for making mistakes, they are usually not mistakes, but opportunities for both of us to get what we want—exceptional and "juicy-on-the dot" life experiences that expand us both infinitely!

None of us is ever bigger or better—we are both the same. Remember that, especially when my respect for you is lacking. Don't shift to meet my disrespect—rather, keep showering me with your respect, so I can learn from you. Please be patient with me!

Let us use our powers of knowing and trusting that we are a team for life and of love, because truthfully it is the exchange between you and me that creates the balance in this life that we get to live together.

If I transition before you, I am not gone—rather, my soul journey in this physical life is complete and your experience of me and with me in your physical life is complete. When you transition, it is the same. Transitioning means that you are complete, that I am complete, and that we as a team are complete —that we initiated in each other exactly what was there for us to initiate, experience, clean out, love, and solve.

I say, let's commit to enjoy this phenomenal physical experience - a gift of love filled with infinite magic - that we are able to provide for each other.

Mom, Dad, get ready! You are about to go on your biggest

and most epic adventure with me. I am excited, over the moon happy, and filled to the brim with love, that I get to BE and live this adventure with you as your child.

Giggles and happy times guaranteed!

I love you more... You can count on it!

—

Your child

THE THREE PILLARS

Just like every sturdy and safe house has some strong pillars ensuring safety and harmony, parenthood has strong pillars that you can practice and live by too—making your parent-child experience a safe, peaceful, and harmonious one!

Here are the pillars:

1. The Harmonious Dance

2. It Is Never The Child

3. The Love Cycle of Parenthood

So let's get to work!

THE HARMONIOUS DANCE
THE FIRST PILLAR

"I am here and ready to dance our harmonious dance together, a flow between two precious souls taking turns being the teacher and the student.

Yes, we take turns…

I am well aware that it seems natural for you to see and feel me as the one who has to be taught and guided, and as the one who does not know that much about life yet.

In some ways that is so, just think of me needing to learn how to brush my teeth and then needing to be reminded to keep doing it. But more often than not I have things to teach to you too—for example, patience.

You ask, "But how do you know what to teach? You are still so young."

Well, that question is pretty silly because as a soul being I have been around and energetically we have access to the same amount of wisdom. I brought that knowing with me into my physical life-job as being your child— entering your life as your student and as your teacher.

So what dance are we dancing?

It's a dance between physical and spiritual because these are entwined parts of life. As long as we flowingly dance in these elements together, we will have a great time. Think about it—"flow" and "dance" carry the energy of ease, softness, being resistance-free and pressure-free, spontaneity, peacefulness yet also vividness, being alive, and plenty of motion. Add "harmonious" to this equation, and we are in for a treat!

I say, let's close our eyes, and imagine that you and I are dancing flowingly and in harmony with each other. This visualization feels amazing, yes?

That's the wonderful feeling that you and I have the power to create in our lives together. It won't always be easy or automatic, but, it is always possible if we spend our time together focusing on dancing in harmony.

One more thing; most often than not, it is really up to you to find your harmony to dance the dance with me, and not the other way around—sorry, but I'm not really sorry!"

~Your Precious Child

In the relationship of parent and child there are two main jobs - two main job openings - that need to be filled and two subjects that really matter—everything else is truly just icing on the cake.

The two jobs, their openings, and their responsibilities are:

1. The teacher job—teacher teaches the student with respect and compassion

2. The student job—student openly allows to be taught and respects the wisdom of their teacher

The two subjects being taught and studied are:

1. Physical Life—all about physical life; eating, showering, using our bodies, sports, playing, human interaction, paying bills…

2. Spiritual Life—all about what's beyond our physical existence; intuition, higher powers, feelings, thoughts, our energetic beings, our soul beings…

These two jobs and two subjects put down the foundation of living and experiencing a soul-fully magical time together with your children—no matter the circumstances, the constellation that your family has, the age groups of your children, or the living situations that are in place.

The important facts about these two jobs and two subjects are:

- Parents and children are both capable of filling either job, the teacher position or the position of being a student—both are here to teach and study the subjects of physical and spiritual. Timing is all that matters.

- One is either the physical teacher making the other the spiritual student, or the spiritual teacher shifting the other to be the physical student—except before having your child/pre-conception, conception/pregnancy, while giving birth, and in transition. For a more in-depth explanation please read the following chapters: Before Having Your Child - Pre-conception, Conception and Pregnancy, Birth, and Transition.

- Both jobs always have to be filled. Any unfilled one will tip the harmonious balance that you both are here to create.

- If both of you are trying to fill the same job it will get too crowded, showing itself as disharmony and discrepancy in family life—parents, you must yield!

- It's up to you as the parent to figure out which job you need to take at which exact moment, and to set an excellent example by giving your best to fulfill the fitting job in a phenomenal and loving way—so your child can copy that.

- If you feel good in your parenting shoes then you are most likely in the right place—versus any of the two jobs being filled by the wrong person at the wrong time will create disharmony.

- When friction arises it's a clear sign that it's time for you to be a flexible and humble parent—re-evaluate which job is yours and change to the rightful one. It's your responsibility!

- Parents must refrain from holding on to a job too long. Your children change at light speed, and most of the time you don't. Focusing on how you feel will alert you ahead of the job-expiration. If you feel good with your children you are perfect where you are. If you don't feel good, it's past time you resign and take up your new job.

How do you know that everyone is occupying the rightful job?

Through the barometer of harmony. When you are the

rightful teacher for the time being, your child will naturally slide into the role of being the student. And when you are the rightful student, your child will happily take the job as your teacher. That IS the harmonious dance for you to flow in, to create harmony with your children.

Keep in mind that the change in the job taking and filling for who the spiritual and who the physical teachers or students are is a constant one, so be on alert Mom and Dad.

Your children are speedsters!

If trouble arises, stop and ask yourself honestly:

"Am I filling the right job right now?"

"Am I studying the right subject right now?"

"Is my child teaching me physically or spiritually right now?"

"Am I dancing a harmonious dance with my child?"

To harmonize, quit the unfitting job that you are holding on for dear life, and with your deepest gratitude, go fill the right and fitting one for right now. No harm done, just a bit of clarity needed and a wonderful adjustment accomplished!

I invite you to dance this "dance of life" with your children in absolute graciousness—meaning, you shift from dancing like you don't know how to dance - creating disharmony - to willingly giving up the lead and learn how to dance WITH your children, accepting them as the respected and equal partner they are - and came forth to BE - in this physical experience called life.

"I did not come here to BE changed—I don't need to BE changed!"

~ Your Child

This IS dancing a harmonious dance with your child!

The stages of parenting, which we will tap into with some examples, are:

- Before Having Your Child: Pre-conception

- Conception and Pregnancy

- Birth

- Baby-hood

- Childhood

- Tween-hood and Teen-hood

- Young Adulthood

- Adulthood

- Transition

BEFORE HAVING YOUR CHILD:
PRE-CONCEPTION

"Yes, there was a time before me. Oh what a glorious time that was, you might think—but no matter how much fun you had in your life before me, it's more fun now, because either I am already here or am about to arrive. And because of me, everything is so much richer in vividness.

I am excited to enjoy through you what you already have experienced, and can't wait to fill the gaps of what you have not experienced yet."

~ *Your Child*

If your child has not arrived in this physical life yet and you are reading this, you have a great advantage, because there is plenty of pre-work that you can do to shift yourself into your best well-feeling before welcoming your bundle of joy, enriching your life, which will spill over into your precious time with your child.

Here is how you can build this nourishing foundation:

- Understand that you are an energetic being having a physical experience

- Acknowledge that you as a whole are a physical body, a mind, a soul, and eternal consciousness

- Keep in mind that everything is energy, connected, and sharing its energies with each other at all times—everything you do, see, hear, taste, smell, think, and feel is energy

- Learn more about energy, vibrations, frequencies, quantum teachings, law of attraction, and what the universe is made of. This knowledge will make your life easier and more joyous while teaching this to your children at a young age is setting them up for a phenomenal life ***

- Live a pressure-free life by letting go of expectations—shifting your experience into an allowing and receiving time. More about this later in the chapter of Loose Ends.

• Live a resistance-free life by acknowledging everyone and everything as IS, followed by accepting, respecting, appreciating, thanking, and loving everyone and everything for the gift and opportunity they ARE, and represent for you. Read in detail about this in the chapter of Loose Ends.

• Create a healthy and happy environment in each of your components—your body, mind, soul, and consciousness. Learn more about this in the chapter of Loose Ends.

If your children already are with you in your physical life, know that it is never too late to start refining and practicing to BE and live at your highest potential—inspiring them to do the same.

*** To get deeper into the teachings of energy, vibrations, frequencies, quantum physics, law of attraction, and what the universe is made of, contact me at FreakyHealer.com ***

No matter if your child was planned, wanted, and/or wished for, there was a time when things were very different in your department of aliveness because your child - or about-to-BE-child - was not in the picture yet. Not saying that before, you were not alive—just a "sorta-kinda," muted alive when you consider the absence of that new playfulness, new childlike sunny outlook, new heart-strong pure love, and the never-ending joyful smiles that arrived for you as soon as that baby was on your horizon. Compare these two times—very different kinds of being alive, when you think of all the action that is knocking, or about to knock, on your door.

When growing the wish to be a parent, you start to shift in many ways. It's automatic! You look at life differently and deeper, you think richer and more thoughtfully, you see yourself and your partner in a different light, you feel your physical body differently, and you start living in a more expanded-feeling way. So before your child even makes it - or made it - into this physical world, they have a huge impact on you. One might say, your child is already turning your whole life upside down. I bet they adore that power!

Considering that they already are with you then, energetically and soul-fully speaking, and are able to influence you so deeply, it is only normal that you are already with them too—energetically and soul-fully speaking. You have the ability to connect with them on an energetic and soul level way before they arrive physically, because remember, we are all energy—making this preparation time a soul-to-soul time.

"In truth, I already had my eyes on you before you even realized that you were pregnant, because I knew that I wanted to have my experience of physical life with you. So I am sitting here in my energetic essence, watching you with delight, peeking at you and your pregnancy preparation process. I know that what you can offer me as your child is exactly what I come here to learn. In exchange, I come with exactly what you want to experience as a parent in your physical life. It really is a win-win exchange that is saturated in the deepest of our love."

~ *Your Child*

Reading the above, doesn't it make you want to pick up the "phone of souls" and connect with your future child right now?

Here is a meditation for connecting with your unborn child:

Sit comfortably in a quiet room—best would be with the doors closed. Close your eyes. Smile. Relax. Start to consciously focus on your breathing. Breathe in and imagine widening your space. Breathe out and imagine letting go of everything. Enjoy this for a little while.

When ready, focus on feeling your energetic being—your light-ness and eternal-ness. Let your energy flow and move by imagining to spread it wide and far into an infinite openness. Consciously feel yourself BE one with everything—a space where you don't feel the outline of your physical body, and a thoughtless-ness that has no memory of your name or what it was that you needed to get at the grocery store. It's like a delightful nothingness!

In that space of being is where you start your connection with your physically unborn child - their soul being - by consciously focusing on feeling their energy, their energetic being, and the pure love and graciousness that they ARE. Feel the sweetness of this "meeting" each other.

Begin chatting with their soul essence. Say hello! Share how you feel about them and how you can't wait to BE together in this physical life. Talk about your love for your child. Thank them for choosing you as the parent and for coming into your physical life experience. Laugh together, and already make plans for the play-time you will have together. Really feel this!

End your beautiful meeting with gratitude!

Beyond meeting energetically you can take this even further, by starting a journal in which you write about how you two will dance in harmony, the feelings you have for your unborn child, your excitement for the grand arrival, the experiences you are planning to have together, and all the laughter and joy that will be. Make this a well-feeling and playful exercise for you! It is supposed to feel good!

Important is that you refrain from writing about how your child will feel, how your child IS, looks, or behaves—that is none of your business because your child has its own reasons and ways to BE and live.

In this pre-conception time your child is both your physical and spiritual teacher, making you a full-time student—spiritually and physically. One of the few exceptions. Spiritually they inspire you to BE a deeper you, while physically you are getting ready to create a physical-life family. Looks like your unborn child is the boss for now! I suggest that you give in and accept this fact by fulfilling your rightful job in this given moment and dancing a harmonious dance with this energetic soul being—your not yet physical child.

"Since I made my choice way before your doubts arose, and before you were stressed, nervous, and on a feeling-roller-coaster ride about being a parent, you can let go of all your unwell feelings and unwell thinkings—they are not needed, not true, and not real! And frankly, it's too late anyways. It's a done deal on my end because the first time I saw you, I fell in love with you."

~ *Your Child*

This is a fantastic time for you to relax about this conceiving business and bringing a baby into this world—you have already been chosen by your child and you have already connected - knowingly or un-knowingly - with the soul being of your child. All that's left for you is to BE and live your happiness. Have fun, be joyous, and take excellent care of your whole being—your body, mind, soul, and your consciousness. Choosing to enjoy your life fully and vividly right now creates a perfect environment for your child to come into—a physical body and a physical life that is happy, healthy, and filled with deep love and joy.

"Mom, Dad, let's face it, I am coming for you and expect to have incredible fun. Thanks for dreaming up and creating your future world of becoming my spectacular Mom and Dad—which is also my future world!"

~ *Your Child*

This IS dancing a harmonious dance with your child!

CONCEPTION — PREGNANCY

Calling this phase *conception* is a funny thing, because it carries the energy of creating something, starting something, or being in charge of making something happen—when all along a beautiful soul contract has already been signed way before the physical conception.

In the physical world it is believed that a child's existence starts with the parents—you know, about the "birds and the bees," and then Mom giving birth after being pregnant. However, as we covered in the pre-conception pages of this book, your child's soul being has already chosen you before arriving here physically, and you might already have made contact with your child on a soul-to-soul level.

"By me choosing you as my perfect parents in this experience of physical life, and by me patiently waiting for you to say "yes" to becoming parents, we finally made this happen!

So ready or not, we are in this together—in conceiving-action now. I will just give you guys privacy, and will sit back with excitement for this phenomenal ME to BE."

~ Your Child

No matter how much love is present in the making of your children, on a soul level they are grateful to be given the possibility to BE here on earth and to experience physical life. Their soul chose this experience exactly as it IS—from start to end!

If there is a lot of love in the making, then way to go! Enjoy and grow this love infinitely by feeling it consciously—making this an expansion of deep love.

"The more conscious you feel the love that is created in the act of my physical conception, the more love you and I get filled with—physically and energetically. The more love you focus on feeling after my conception, the fuller

my love tank gets, and so does yours! And the fuller our tanks are, the more relaxed and peaceful it is for me to be and grow inside of you—making me your absolute bundle of love once I pop out into the world!"

~ *Your Child*

If there is not - or was not - a huge amount of love involved, remember that even in the absence of it, you are giving the gift of physical life to a soul who wants to come into this physical world —who actually has made its strong-willed choice to arrive.

Freeing yourself of pressure that feels like there was not, or is not, enough love is crucial, because that unwell-feeling energy fills every single cell of your whole being with un-wellness— sharing it with your unborn child.

By shifting your focus onto the beautiful fact that you are giving a precious soul the gift of physical life, you create the love you thought was not previously there, or not there enough.

"I AM created, and that is enough for now! Let's love that fact!"

~ *Your Child*

This creation-experience awakens powerful mechanisms in your physical body that you never experienced before. Spiritually, you are finding yourself on a grander love and wisdom plateau than you have ever stood on. Let's settle with "You are growing out the roof here!" That is why in the conception phase and during pregnancy, your physically developing child is your spiritual and your physical teacher—and you are a student in both the physical and the spiritual classes. One of the few exceptions.

Your job is:

"To already talk and connect with me, right now!"

~ *Your Child*

And to:

• Nourish yourself in a way that always holds the health of your body - the physical home of your unborn child - and your mind, your soul and your consciousness, in the highest regard —through feeling what is best for you, following what feels right for you, and by asking your soul being because it always knows. Your unborn child's soul being helps you with this through signals of cravings, new feelings, and inspired well-being, and will share with you their well-being-state when there is lack of healing or a need for reparation in your physical body.

• Nourish yourself with anything and anyone that feels joyful, playful, and happy for you—shifting yourself into an energetic environment that is filled by your deep knowing, lots of humor, and plenty of laughter. The perfect stage for you and your unborn child to grow and glow.

This IS dancing a harmonious dance with your child!

BIRTH

"In the experience of giving birth, we are two souls whom in a spectacular togetherness start the physical journey of parent-child-hood."

~ Your Child!

In the birthing phase your child stays to be your full-time teacher, physically and spiritually, keeping you glued to the hot seat as a full-time student of all. One of the few exceptions.

Physically, you experience a strength that you never knew you had. A pain which, created by giving birth, then immediately turns into the love of your life - your new baby - and an overwhelmingly excited feeling to welcome your child, who is blessed to take its first breath of air on this earth.

Hopefully you, beautiful Mom, will also take a proud peek at your limitless physical body after you catch your breath and receive your first skin-touching moment with your precious child. This is your moment of glory! So in fullness and graciousness, exchange the sweetest welcome with your newborn child—physically and spiritually.

"I want to thank you Mom! Coming through your womb was quite the adventure. I am new! I am fresh! I am here to find my way deep into my soul being and to follow my soul calling."

~ Your Child

Spiritually, you are invited to really comprehend this magnificent event and dive deep into your soul—knowing that all of physical life is indeed very spiritual, that you are very spiritual, and that your child is a spiritual being first and foremost. This is a phenomenal initiation for you to shift to BE and live your soul being and to connect deeply to your soul calling.

Studying hard and beautifully is all that I can recommend!

As to what's next, I think you know exactly what to do—cuddle, hug, stare, and do what feels phenomenal for you and your newborn child. Savor this sacred pleasure of you and your child for as long as possible in solitude. Close the windows, lock the doors, and disconnect the the phones—this harmonious time is meant for you, your child, and your family. Everyone else's time will come soon enough, whenever you are ready to share.

Bravo, you are already so good at this "harmonious dance" with your child!

"Hi Mom! Hi Dad! Finally, we get to meet in person!

I hope that by now, you are already in total unconditional love with me. But here is the deal; in case you are not or are struggling to feel that love, I want you to not worry or create pressure that you have to feel it right now. Nor do I want you to think that something is wrong. Our love is not based on how much we feel it for each other at any given moment—our love just IS! So no matter the circumstances - tired, feeling empty, not ourselves or being in disharmony - our love IS real and IS always here. Glad we got that out of the way, because besides smiling at you, I will give you trouble, make your life harder, and even make you cry at times. Plenty of ups and downs are coming for us—during those times you and I can always remember that our love just IS, that our love IS real, and IS always here. So let's not do pressure, have no have to's, and certainly not create any struggles. I love you already!"

~ Your Child

This IS dancing a harmonious dance with your child!

BABY-HOOD

"I awaken in you feelings that nourish you on a very deep level. Be consciously aware of these strong love-feelings—feel them fully."

~ Your Child

When your child is a baby you are mostly the physical teacher, teaching your student all that you can about this physical life. That is because your child is a real newbie to this and doesn't know anything about physical life yet—besides automatically breathing, crying, peeing, and pooping.

"You teach me everything in this physical world right - eating, smiling, hearing, and making pleasant noises - and fill me with feelings of safety, being cared for and being loved. In return, I am initiating and growing in you a new love—you have never loved this purely, this deeply, and this beautifully before."

~ Your Child

Spiritually, it's mostly your baby's turn to teach you, so hold your spiritual horses for now!

You are the spiritual student at this time because your baby awakens in you a spiritual depth that you did not have before and brings new spiritual experiences into your life. This spiritual teaching and spiritual initiating originates from the cleanest and purest place of "being" ever - a new baby who has not yet been tainted by any experiences of physical life - whereas what you bring to the table is contaminated with dusty old experiences. Yes, you have been around for a while and formed some real unfitting and untruthful beliefs, but remember; in your soul existence you are just like your baby - pure and clean - meaning, only in your physical existence does your dust exist.

So get that energetic duster out and start dusting—by shifting yourself to BE and live in your pure and clean soul essence.

Here is a "dust-be-gone" meditation:

Sit comfortably in a quiet room—best would be with the doors closed. Close your eyes. Smile. Relax. Start to consciously focus on your breathing. Breathe in and imagine widening your space. Breathe out and imagine letting go of everything. Enjoy this for a little while.

When ready, focus on feeling your energetic being—your light-ness and eternal-ness. Let your energy flow and move by imagining to spread it wide and far into an infinite openness. Consciously feel yourself BE one with everything—a space where you don't feel the outline of your physical body, and a thoughtless-ness that has no memory of your name or what it was that you needed to clean or get done. It's like a delightful nothingness!

In that space of being is where you can connect with your dust-free being, your deep love, your infinite graciousness, and the pure positively squeaky-clean soul essence that you ARE. Feel the sweetness of this!

End your beautiful meeting with gratitude!

Once in your soul space, digest your baby's spiritual teachings and turn them into the highest and purest form of expansion for yourself. This newborn love that you feel for your baby will carry you far, energize you limitlessly, heal your own baby traumas, and will let you go through life as a bigger you, a more you, and as an expanded truth of who you really are—your eternal soul being.

"I want to tell you that...

...You are perfect!

...You are enough!

...You are lovable!

...You are loved!

...You are beautiful!

...You are my perfect MOM and DAD!

There is nothing - when given from your heart and with your pure love - that you can do wrong. Just love me, teach me, accept my teachings, and enjoy this sacred time of us together! Let's take every moment as it comes and live it as it IS—perfect."

~ Your Child

Keep in mind that the change in the job taking and filling for who the spiritual and who the physical teachers or students are is a constant one, so be on alert Mom and Dad.

Your children are speedsters!

If trouble arises, stop and ask yourself honestly:

"Am I filling the right job right now?"

"Am I studying the right subject right now?"

"Is my child teaching me physically or spiritually right now?"

"Am I dancing a harmonious dance with my child?"

To harmonize, quit the unfitting job that you are holding on for dear life, and with your deepest gratitude, go fill the right and fitting one for right now. No harm done, just a bit of clarity needed and a wonderful adjustment accomplished!

This IS dancing a harmonious dance with your child!

CHILDHOOD

"I am in my busy body years! Let's play! I can walk, jump, run—and run away. Come find me—I am playing hide and seek with you! Read a book to me! And yes, I ask endless questions... Have patience with me when I keep you on your tippy toes—as I practice patience with you too!"

~ Your Child

These busy years shift your child often to be your physical teacher, making you the physical student—just think of physically keeping up with this constant and fast movement. Old beliefs of being always tired, and "it's too much," or "I have to rest," limit a parent's energetic expansion immensely while being tested on a physical level by trying to keep up—not to mention all of the experiences that go un-felt by living these old limits.

Just as an athlete trains and constantly finds new personal records, you going after your children with an attitude originating from your bottom-less soul will help you find new personal physical records that are beyond what you believed were possible in the first place.

I say, "Study hard!" and go play with them!

That gives you the spiritual teaching job—making your child your faithful spiritual student. You teach about behavior, kindness, gratitude, appreciation, worth, and help create their beliefs, in this physical stage of life.

"I might not always like what you are saying and sometimes I don't even want to hear it—hence my rebelliousness. When I am testing your beliefs, your ways, and your words, you can re-feel them and either take an even stronger stand, or come to the conclusion that what you are saying is not in alignment with what's true for you either. Both ways is a big win, because in one you will strengthen your clarity and in the other, you inch closer to who you really are."

~ Your Child

Keep in mind that the change in the job taking and filling for who the spiritual and who the physical teachers or students are is a constant one, so be on alert Mom and Dad.

Your children are speedsters!

If trouble arises, stop and ask yourself honestly:

"Am I filling the right job right now?"

"Am I studying the right subject right now?"

"Is my child teaching me physically or spiritually right now?"

"Am I dancing a harmonious dance with my child?"

To harmonize, quit the unfitting job that you are holding on for dear life, and with your deepest gratitude, go fill the right and fitting one for right now. No harm done, just a bit of clarity needed and a wonderful adjustment accomplished!

This IS dancing a harmonious dance with your child!

TWEEN-HOOD AND TEEN-HOOD

"As a tweener and teenager I need you immensely and I want your help, but not the way you want to give it to me. So please adjust yourself, expand with light-speed, and give me your help, but my way."

~ *Your Tweener and Teenager*

Moving into the strong-felt teenage years, the job and subject changing is constant!

Sometimes it changes in split seconds—making it exhausting for parents because they are usually not up to speed with their teenagers and their expansion that is orbiting with light speed. Makes sense when you think of the stability that parents are giving their best to create, and to hold on to, in their physical-life jobs to make a living and to provide for their family.

However, if a clear separation of the physical and spiritual happenings is in place, then this light-speed of energetic change that is inspired by your teenagers should not be hard to adjust to. Your teenager is never expecting you to copy this constant change of expansion into your physical life—so keep your stability in your physical lives going while taking this wild ride of expanding on your soul-level fully. Yeehaw!

In a perfect world it would go something like this:

Your teenager - bookworm or athlete - is your physical teacher because they go through a lot of physical change. They show you how they deal with physicality - body, sexuality, and sleep to name a few - in their own new, fresh, and young ways, inspiring you to heal and touch up your own teenage feelings for yourself. Pay attention and study hard!

Many teenagers are also modeling for you how much they can do physically in these strong, powerful, and young years—support all sportive activities and try to match their athletic capabilities. You will be surprised at how much you thought you can't do anymore, but actually can. What a huge win for - and in - your physical expansion!

This makes you the spiritual teacher! But this time the job is much harder, because you can't teach your teenager by telling them—only by demonstrating and practicing your being of your spiritual soul-self, and then successfully living it, can you teach your teenager to BE and live their true soul calling too. For instance, loving yourself IS teaching your teenager the spiritual meaning of self-love.

This might be the hardest teaching job you ever had, but for one, you are capable, and two, the success-feeling of it is huge! So lower your head, push through, and perform like an olympic winner!

"I am growing my own kingdom here. Can't you see? Leave me alone and get out of my way! Sayings things like that is my constant guidance for you that you are not showing up as your expanded version of your soul trueness, but rather, are giving me your not-expanded soul version—that is why I am rebelling and will continue to rebel until you expand to who you really are. I want to meet as my newly expanded me with your newly expanded you!"

~ Your Tweener and Teenager

When feeling down or maybe even at the edge of the abyss because of your teenagers, realize that it has nothing to do with them. Instead, you went on a trip down your own teenage memory lane—into your own strong-feeling teenage years.

Take this opportunity to learn!

Welcome these hard patches of parenting your teenagers with the conscious understanding that they exist because your reactions towards your teenagers come from your old beliefs and your own mostly unresolved teenage experiences—not from your true expanded soul being of pure positive energy that you are. Otherwise, there would be no hard patch.

During a time like this it is best to make a hard turn to get out of your teenager's way. Once out of sight, acknowledge this happening with humbleness and take it as a great release and healing opportunity—to heal yourself on your own teenage level.

When back in alignment with who you really are and feeling like you can fulfill the spiritual job that you have right now, turn around and face your teenager with reactions coming from your pure soul-level—making this a pure positive soul-to-soul exchange.

"Your teachings in this time come from me watching how you are being and living—I secretly admire you when you are your expanded version because your well-feeling and happiness is inspiring and contagious!"

~ Your Teenager

Let's talk about stillness!

Less words and barely any questions, from the parent, are key in these sensitive years when your teenagers are building, creating, and realizing themselves—fulfilling their needs, supporting their dreams, loving them unconditionally, and respecting them with your infinite trust is the biggest confidence boost that you can give them.

Sitting in silence with them means it's physically quiet, but energetically you have this huge power of showering and filling them to the brim - and into overflow - with your complete admiration and knowing of their limitless soul beings. Remember, your feelings are energy, and all energies are always shared with others—how you feel about them is what you share with them, spread to them, and what you fill them with. That IS how much power you have—in silence!

"When I don't want to talk to you it does not mean that I don't want to spend time with you, I just don't want to talk —meaning, I want to be with your energy and not with your words. And even though that might seem like a low impact, low influential, or a non-supporting role, it is the most powerful support that you can give me right now—especially if your feelings

about me are of a positive, believing, trusting, and loving nature."

~ *Your Tweener and Teenager*

To take it even further...

When you are in a state of being, you are in a space where nothing has to be and nothing has to happen—the purest energetic soul space ever. Now imagine that you are being in that silent nothing-space with your teenager, as two souls, hanging out —sharing, spreading, and connecting as ONE and the same. That IS how powerful - and many times purer - quiet time can BE.

"Sometimes I come to tease you. That means that I am showing you my love for you through my playful-ness! Please don't tease me back all the time - I can be sensitive - instead just go with me teasing you, and laugh with me."

~ *Your Tweener and Teenager*

When your teenager says "Mom, Dad, we have to move on from this!" take it seriously! Be a nice and compliant parent and move on!

When they say things like that, it is a great reality checker on where you stand with your thoughts, feelings, and energy, because most likely you are desperately hanging onto something of unwell-feeling nature that already was—making the momentum of said unwanted feeling bigger and bigger. Welcome any "Move on!" your child says to you as an it's-about-time alarm for you to shift out of being stuck and into your freedom.

In my opinion, these words are one of the greatest gifts that your teenagers can give you—even if they are not consciously aware, they can feel you being stagnant, meaning that they have your back. So move on!

"Sometimes you are my punching bag, which is probably not a fun job for you. I don't mean to hurt you - because remember, I do love you deeply - but that is the best I can do right now. So please, don't engage, and if you have to, push back gently, because I am hurting too. Thank you for

understanding!"

~ Your Tweener and Teenager

Before encountering your teenagers make sure that you are in your well-feeling state, your soul being. Meditate, feed yourself first, hug yourself first, and do whatever it takes to create the perfect stage to BE with your child—a stage that will let everyone's stars shine.

This leaves fighting with your teenager out of the equation because when you are deeply connected with yourself you will see them as your soul sees them—pure positive energy. That way you have a fair chance to know and understand your teenager's needs, which is a huge gift since knowing what a teenager really needs or wants is many times a seemingly impossible guessing-game and changes second to second.

If you can't figure out what is desired, a "thank you" - find something, anything, that you can say thank you for - and trying later is always better than asking questions at the wrong time. Most likely your teenager doesn't know what the need is either. Think of it like asking a person why they are vomiting and are feeling sick in their stomach, while they are vomiting. They most likely don't know - and don't care - the why or what, making them frustrated and the question unhelpful. And the vomiting? It's still happening!

If you do know the desire, graciously allow yourself to adapt to your teenager's needs and don't be surprised if you find that you also nurture your own desires by doing so. To some of you, this might seem a bit like spoiling your children, but that is not true! Remember, you are "dancing a harmonious dance" together! Your time together is an exchange; sometimes you fill your children's desires, also nurturing your own desires, and sometimes it is the opposite—your child fills your desires while also filling their own desires.

Plus, why not let your children's desires lead since desires are always pure soul callings?

"As for sharing information about my life, my friends, and my love experiences... It's very simple! I share what I want to share. If you have questions, and really really really can't lay them to rest, ask them as generally as you can. Please forgive me if my answers are not as polite as you want them to be. I don't intend to be mean, I just love to ferociously protect my privacy—to BE me. Sometimes my life gets really overwhelming and it's difficult to turn all my experiences into good words, words that I am fine sharing with you. In those times I ask you to trust in me and my capabilities, in my knowing, and in my natural instinct. I got this and I got my life! Your trust, support, quiet guidance, and belief in me nourishes my roots to BE me, and a lot of times cleanses my confusion of becoming a mature physical being. Plus, let's be honest here, the less you ask, the more I will freely share with you."

~ *Your Tweener and Teenager*

When you believe that things need to be fixed with your teenagers - in their lives and with their friends - know that you are in the wrong by crossing soul boundaries. Nothing and nobody has to be fixed—ever! Yet, your tweeners and teenagers need to be unconditionally supported and quietly guided, by you —their way.

Keep in mind that the change in the job taking and filling for who the spiritual and who the physical teachers or students are is a constant one, so be on alert Mom and Dad.

Your children are speedsters!

If trouble arises, stop and ask yourself honestly:

"Am I filling the right job right now?"

"Am I studying the right subject right now?"

"Is my child teaching me physically or spiritually right now?"

"Am I dancing a harmonious dance with my child?"

To harmonize, quit the unfitting job that you are holding on for dear life, and with your deepest gratitude, go fill the right and fitting one for right now. No harm done, just a bit of clarity needed and a wonderful adjustment accomplished!

This IS dancing a harmonious dance with your child!

YOUNG ADULTHOOD

"So here we are—ME being my own adult ME, but all you can see is me being your little baby!" ~ Your Young Adult

What a magical time it was when your child was little!

Breathe this wonderful memory in for a minute and feel that well-feeling as alive and as vivid, as it was just yesterday—filling every single cell of your whole being - body, mind, soul, consciousness - with wellness.

For your child it was magical too. It was a playful phase of life, while learning from you and the surroundings that were present and watching it all unfold—yet also fulfilling the job of being your highest teacher in many ways.

Naturally, you are driven to hold on to those times - that playfulness and that magic - because you miss that, and you miss those babies and those little children. Rightfully so—but there are different ways of holding on, and some are better than others!

Imagine holding on to a beautiful keepsake while remembering and re-feeling the magic, versus holding on to a bumper of a speeding car that is trying to flee the scene. Yikes! Big difference there.

If you are holding on to seeing and feeling your child as being little, you are showering them with an energy that is not fitting for who they are now—creating an unwell feeling for you and your young adult, unwell because it is not their - or your - truth anymore. This will show itself by your young adult not feeling respected as an adult and by you experiencing a very short-lived good feeling, then wondering where the heck it went. Holding on to the bumper here!

The better way to hold on to that wonderful time is for you to re-see, re-hear, re-talk, re-smell, re-taste, re-think, and re-feel the joy - and not the child - that saturated said time, while focusing on respecting your young adult as the grownup they are now. This creates the most wonderful co-creation because you can spend time as two adult people, talking about the fun you both had back then—harmony at its best.

This proves that you don't ever have to miss anything, because you can re-create exactly what you miss anytime and anywhere by re-visiting the feelings of what you miss—filling your gap right then and there. Just think of the keepsake mentioned earlier, that IS how much power you possess.

Some parents connect having grown children with them feeling older, meaning they put the realization and unwell-feeling of being older onto having a young adult. A very weighed-down way of parenting. So stop that, one has nothing to do with the other, because "older" only connects with how old you feel yourself being in your physical ways.

And some, hopefully you, might bathe in your absolute pride of being the parent of such an amazing young adult person - a beautiful soul who IS living their truth - without taking the credit, because they choose to BE that!

Meeting your young adult right where they are - not little anymore and not wanting to be little anymore - means with that new focus comes new adventures for you to experience together. And who knows, you might even take the brave leap to sit back and let this amazing young person tell you how the world works, and how they see it through those sharp young adult eyes. Imagine all the fresh-ness that is born with that heroic act of yours and the making of an incredibly better earth that we get to BE and live in.

"In this phase of our glorious parent-child-relationship, we compliment each other in a constant change of being the physical or the spiritual teacher and student. One moment it's this way and the other moment it's that way… Never a dull moment, so stay alert Mom and Dad!"

~ Your Young Adult

So…

Keep in mind that the change in the job taking and filling for who the spiritual and who the physical teachers or students are is a constant one, so be on alert Mom and Dad.

Your children are speedsters!

If trouble arises, stop and ask yourself honestly:

"Am I filling the right job right now?"

"Am I studying the right subject right now?"

"Is my child teaching me physically or spiritually right now?"

"Am I dancing a harmonious dance with my child?"

To harmonize, quit the unfitting job that you are holding on for dear life, and with your deepest gratitude, go fill the right and fitting one for right now. No harm done, just a bit of clarity needed and a wonderful adjustment accomplished!

This IS dancing a harmonious dance with your child!

ADULTHOOD

"Now that I am older, I understand many things about the what, how, and why of your actions when I was growing up—actions that highlighted my emotions of anger and frustration. I really need to let you off the hook in many of those situations because I get it now, that you too, where giving your best. Do I see a smirk?"

~ *Your Adult*

The further along you get to go with your children in this physical life, the richer it gets to BE for the both of you. Through their own adult experiences outside of your house, sight, and ears, and through having their own children - making your adult children hard studying students - they turn to BE your most profound spiritual teachers ever. They are passing the new learned spiritual freshness that is shifting them into their new - wanted or not - expansion of being adults, to you. Accept this as a gift! By doing so, you are choosing to allow your own immense beautiful expansion that you are so "high time" ready for.

In turn, you shift to being the physical teacher. You have reached a time where it is of greatest importance to take excellent care of your physical body and physical life, in order to BE, live, and stay healthy for a long time—to enjoy the new-found freedom for a long time.

At other times, you are their spiritual teacher. Through having experienced many diverse phases of life and through staying awake plenty of nights by thinking "What could I have done better or differently?" you have endless soul wisdom to give and share.

Remember though, re-feeling and re-guilting those insecure moments will not help you or your adult child. On the contrary, it creates unwell feelings between the two of you—and all that, over old and untrue things. You did the best you could with what you knew at that time and with what you had back then. That IS always true for everyone, period!

When you acknowledge these spiritual understandings on your soul level, and turn them into your most precious practice of well-feeling in your now, that is when you are teaching your adult child to BE and live on a deep spiritual level; not to mention the emotional cleansing, healing, and the huge shift to happiness that takes place. Your grown-up child then turns to BE your physical teacher—showing you new ways to live, exercise, eat, pamper, and love yourself. Let's face it, times have changed, new methods and ideas are born, and new expansions ARE on every level. Let their teachings take you to the top of the mountain of wellbeing!

Keep in mind that the change in the job taking and filling for who the spiritual and who the physical teachers or students are is a constant one, so be on alert Mom and Dad.

Your children are speedsters!

If trouble arises, stop and ask yourself honestly:

"Am I filling the right job right now?"

"Am I studying the right subject right now?"

"Is my child teaching me physically or spiritually right now?"

"Am I dancing a harmonious dance with my child?"

To harmonize, quit the unfitting job that you are holding on for dear life, and with your deepest gratitude, go fill the right and fitting one for right now. No harm done, just a bit of clarity needed and a wonderful adjustment accomplished!

This IS dancing a harmonious dance with your child!

TRANSITION

"When a soul essence leaves the physical body it is never lost, gone, done with, or not present anymore. Graciousness, a soul, IS eternal."

~ Your Child

When a being transitions back to its energetic non-physical existence, it means there were enough experiences that were lived or enough life that was experienced. "Enough" in the sense of "I am fulfilled. I am complete. I AM!"—no matter the circumstances of the transition or the age of the one who is transitioning. This is a perfectly beautiful time to shift homeward, to eternal soul-graciousness, also, the essence of pure positive energy.

If you are transitioning before your child, you are clearly an enormous spiritual teacher in this emotional happening by firing up feelings that - even though they were in your and your child's presences all along - are now surfacing to BE felt and lived.

You have incredible power in this time to influence your child in the way you speak about your experience of transitioning, and also in the way you feel about it—when you are conscious about your shift into the non-physical. You are spreading and sharing the energy that you are vibrating in—feeling negative and sad influences your child in a heavy way, while feeling grateful and gracious about this phase of your life shifts your child into a deep spiritual graciousness.

There is a lot to come to peace with - on the physical and non-physical level - in such a meaningful time of physical life for both the one transitioning and the one staying.

When felt mostly - or only - on the physical life level it can be an overwhelmingly painful experience, because as such, it is based on losing someone and searching for reasons, until the one left behind gives in from a point of exhaustion and unwell-feeling.

When felt on the soul-level it is experienced through the foundation of our deep inner knowing that nobody is ever losing anyone, that we are all energy, and are always connected with each other at all times and in all forms.

Allow yourself to freely feel every feeling that you have and welcome them all as an important part of you—shifting everything that you feel to BE a gift that inches you closer and closer to who you really are. From there, soothe your hurting heart by embracing the expansion on your soul level.

In this time there is no need for your child to teach you physically, your energetic being is calling you into its arms and loving space. Your child can rest.

Yet, there is a beautiful profoundness that you can gift your child with:

If you are consciously looking at your child in their physical form and embrace the evoked heartfelt gratitude and appreciation for the health and sturdiness of their physical presence, you create a deep and grand love - for you to feel - before transitioning. When consciously felt by you, this infinite love is spread and shared with your child—filling both of your whole beings.

Love IS the grandest potency of healing, because love originates from your heart, the host of your pure positive essence —your soul. Touched by that love? You are either residing in, or being shifted into, your gracious soul space of who you really are.

If your child transitions before you, your child is your spiritual and your physical life teacher. One of the few exceptions.

Spiritually, your child's experience of transitioning asks you to go deep into your soul being to find the strength to fulfill this meaningful time graciously. A deep soul-knowing and soul-feeling that you are not losing your child is available for you to tap into, because energetically all is eternal.

On the physical life level, that is all based on touching, holding, and witnessing your child's physical body, the pain of your child's transition can be immense. The invitation here is for you to find your soothing moments by shifting unconditionally to BE and live in your soul being, and live life through that for a while—creating physical wellness. Because to feel, to understand, and to live this emotional time through your physical life level is simply too painful right now and can create physical un-wellness —whereas lived soul-fully, it is a beautiful completion of moving into your soul essence, where you ARE closest to yourself and where you ARE closest to the energetic essence of your child, their soul being.

"It's me, Mom and Dad! I am still here! I can still tease and love you— only now, without being seen or caught. It's me! I AM always with you!"

~Your Child

This IS dancing a harmonious dance with your child!

IT'S NEVER THE CHILD
THE SECOND PILLAR

"What's really interesting, is that nowhere does it say how to really do the physical experience of parent-child-hood! We just have to find our own ways to co-exist in absolute well-feeling—a harmony that helps me and helps you. A co-creation of our true wave of love that is shared and spread to everyone and everything, everywhere—helping the whole world and beyond."

~ *Your Child*

Things really come into perspective when you take a step back and focus on what your children really are—beautiful soul beings who come into this physical life with the expectation to fulfill their purpose of being. That's it!

What does that mean?

They are here not to impress anyone, anything, life itself, or you—but to BE themselves and only to BE themselves. Oh wait… Funny, it's the same for you!

"I too am here as a soul, in a body, to experience this physical existence for - and as - myself. I am not here to follow you blindly or to learn only from your experiences that are based on your ways of living your life. I made the trek here to experience my destiny, my way, and my life—together with you."

~ *Your Child*

Misbehaving—that's what we call it when a child acts out, right?

When children misbehave, it's like a complete fog surrounds the parents until they can't see anything anymore. The reason for why the children are here in the first place is completely forgotten, unknown, and un-remembered—or else it would not be called misbehaving. Rather we would roar with pride, "They are behaving accordingly to their heart's desire."

A child always behaves suitably and in the most truthful and fitting ways to their own soul-calling. Any of those given naughty moments are the most important times for parents to look clearly, but not at the children; rather, at themselves, their own feelings, their own energy they are being and living, and what profound wisdom is being amplified for them.

If the behavior of a child is delightful for the parent, then the child's soul calling is in alignment with the parents' expectations —a wonderful happening if that is the case. Enjoy freely!

"I want to learn from you and I want to listen to you, but only if it's in alignment with my journey and my soul calling that I am here to BE and live."

~ *Your Child*

However, if the child misbehaves it is not a misbehavior at all, only a difference in what the parent wants and what the child wants - and follows to stay truthful - in their soul calling— showing up to the parent as trouble, issues, and problems.

Calling this "trouble" is very inaccurate, and not at all fair to the child since they are here in this physical life to follow their soul calling—even if it is not in alignment with the parents' expectations.

To take this even further, a lot of parents' expectations originate from old beliefs, old have-to's, and antique out-of-style ways, not from their true, new, and modern soul-being they are today—hence the saying, "It was always done that way!" Every child's misbehavior is a wonderful chance that is filled with wisdom and learning, clearly showing that Mom and Dad are not being and living their up-to-date truth and joy.

So, who is really misbehaving here?

- If your children happen to respect and allow their own knowing then your children are behaving—behaving as their soul beings are telling them to do. Nice children!

- If you happen to respect and allow the fact that they are following their soul calling, then you as a parent are behaving —behaving as your soul being is telling you to see your children and the situation. Nice parent!

Every soul is here to BEhave as themselves—making the above picture one that is in heavenly order.

When things are going great with your children and you feel excited about their behavior it is easy to say, "My kids are nice!" You want to make sure that these words originate truly from your soul being, who has the child's heart desire in best interest. Differentiate such a moment into two piles:

- Children are nicely doing as I say, even if it does not fit for them

- Children are nicely behaving because both our soul-callings are matching up at this moment

You will know the difference between the two by checking in with how everyone is feeling—if all of you are behaving accordingly to your true beings, then there is nothing but joy present.

But what about boasting? If you are in a great place, meaning you are deeply connected to your soul being, then the statement of "My kids are nice!" is one of pureness, and should be indulged in, shared, and spread with your children and beyond, meaning publicly—this comes from you, is only about you, and is because of your connection to your soul being! If not, refrain from indulging in this "fake" and short-lived goodness that is only going to annoy your children. Look inward first—get yourself back on track by being and living your truth, and only then share and spread.

Refrain from suggesting that your children are the issue! When you are not feeling excited, or not wanting to shout out to the whole world and beyond that your children are your heroes, look at where you stand with yourself, how you feel, what energy you are in, and how far off from your true you, you really are. Remember:

- It is never your children's job to make you feel good, feel honored, feel respected, and to give you reasons to say "My kids are the best!"

- It is also never your children's job to behave to your liking!

But it is your job to get your physical bottom back into the vicinity of your soul being, where you feel good for yourself and about yourself - on your own and without your children's help - no matter the circumstances or the quality of the relationship with your children.

This way of parenting shifts you into a true space of knowing that no matter what your children are doing, you are soul-grown enough to separate your behavior and feelings from their behaviors—meaning you are taking full responsibility and excellent care of your own feelings.

In no way do I suggest that this is an easy and automatic task, but with commitment, practice, and passionate self-soul-love it is possible—and also the only way to **Parent Through The Eyes of Lollipops**, through the eyes of your soul being.

"Having to make Mom and Dad feel good is a really heavy weight to carry!"

~ Your Child

If you would give "behaving for someone else" a form, it would be something like a huge boulder. Asking or demanding that your children behave for you means you load that huge boulder on their backs for them to carry while they play, run, and develop into who they really are—not a lighthearted sight at all.

"It is never the child! It is never the child's fault—and it is never the child's job to fix it!"

~ Your Child

To recap, when your children rebel it has meaning. One, they are following their soul calling, which we covered above. Two, your child is mirroring you something that you are ready to see, feel, heal, realize, and take responsibility of.

"When trouble arises, I am your mirror! Look into it!"

~ Your Child

Your children are the greatest and most beautiful truth mirrors ever! They un-dig what is in perfect timing for you to look at—the beautiful, the okay, and the ugly. Parents, get ready —the ugly is what grabs your undivided attention as this undeniable feeling, "My child is being bad!"

When it's almost like your children:

• Think it is their job to teach you—oh wait, it IS!

• Have this inner knowing of what to teach you—oh wait, they do!

Don't worry, I got you covered. Here is a gracious, loving, and harmonious way to handle any iffy situation with your children—with guaranteed soul-expansion:

• Allow this situation as your mirror

• Ask, "What does this have to do with me?"

• Ask yourself, "What is my child mirroring for me?"

• Feel your feelings about this situation

• Take full responsibility for how you feel

Acknowledge all of the information that you receive through the above checklist freely and openly. From there, accept, respect, appreciate, thank, and love the huge gift of shifting to BE and live in your soul-knowing.

And poof, it's like magic, immediately your child's rebellion can vanish because the mirroring job is done. They can turn their back on being your mirror in this situation—releasing them into infinite freedom to move on, until their next mirroring duty calls. Lucky you to have such a nice big mirror!

"How you feel has nothing to do with me! When you feel tired, you are not tired because of me; when you are hurt, you are not hurt because of me; when you are sad, you are not sad because of me. Your feelings are always yours and my feelings are always mine."

~ *Your Child*

If the rebellion is not blowing over with you taking responsibility of your feelings, know that this situation is a mixture of the child being your mirror and their own learning and expansion. Once you take over what's yours, your child can then experience their own part purely and freely—making this experience a true soul expansion for all.

"You cannot make me feel better by taking over my feelings, because my feelings are not your responsibility—but you can make me feel better by loving me unconditionally as I am."

~ *Your Child*

This harmonious flow works for any imbalance; be it tantrums, school issues, trouble with other kids, or chores. It's never, ever, your child's fault!

"Of course, if it happens - and it will - that I am disrespectful, then guide me, teach me, and support me. My actions are my actions and I want to be responsible for them—even if I don't agree with that right now. However, I cannot take responsibility for how you feel about my actions."

~ *Your Child*

Think of you and your child having the same goal - to experience a truthful soul-expansion in this physical life - but wanting to take different directions to get there.

Sometimes these different directions are very close—maybe even side by side. Sometimes they are worlds apart. Sometimes they meet, and sometimes they don't. Most importantly though, they all point to the one and only reason of our physical existence here—to BE truthful to our soul being.

If you make your children switch to the direction that you choose, they are not able to experience what would have been experienced had they stayed on their originally chosen path—making your path not-chosen and un-fitting for them. That wrong direction shows up through them being rebellious, because your children know that the direction is where all the personal soul expansion is created.

"Sure, I am stubborn and I know that I come across as such, but that stubbornness is me defending my path, me sticking up for my path, and me trying to communicate with you that what you are wanting from me is not my path. I am hoping that you will understand and not ask me to walk a path that is yours—one unfitting for me to walk."

~ Your Child

Don't make your children change the direction that they chose—especially not because you believe the other way is better for them.

Not only does this make them get off their soul-course, if you are focused on making them change your way, you are not truly moving in your own direction either. The result being, none of you are expanding truly into who you really are. Stay on your course and let them stay on their course, and if needed, be there for them to have their backs—without leaving your own path.

This lets you keep a clean, orderly, and organized house—or shall we say soul. Living in the same house but sleeping in separate rooms shows you how you can live in the same physical life time, yet experience and expand in different ways—by separating responsibilities, capabilities, all feelings, and all preferred ways, you each get to decorate your own digs the way you like, making it a life you really want to BE and live in—one that belongs to you.

"I do not have to be molded, I do not have to be changed, and I do not have to be made different. I am perfect as IS."

~ *Your Child*

It's guaranteed that all of you hit the jackpot of physical life this way and will return back home - to your soul - with a full bucket of wins at the end. Because let's be real here, everyone who is given their own free space can BE and live to their highest potential.

This IS Parenting Through the Eyes of Lollipops!

THE LOVE CYCLE OF PARENTHOOD
THE THIRD PILLAR

"The love that a parent feels for their child IS real! The love that a child feels for their parents IS real! Are we good and clear on that?"

~ Your Child

It is with utmost pleasure, a bit of a giggle, and infinite excitement, to know that the above is very obvious and that we agree that the arrival and existence of a child IS the grandest love that has ever been initiated—in you and for you.

You can't hide from that fact, that happening, that learning, and that deep inner knowing—let alone that love. Might as well give in to this high-for-life feeling of "I love my children into infinity and back." Actually, just pack your bag of feelings and move into that frequency to stay and never leave again. What a perfect way to live this physical parenting life!

If this grand love is not being felt by you at this moment, know that there is nothing wrong with you or your children, and that this love is not and never will be absent—on the contrary, this grand love is a guaranteed essence of being a parent and its initiation is automatic. You just can't feel it in your physical person at the moment. If you would solely see, think, hear, taste, smell, and feel through your soul being - versus your physical being - you would be shown that your love for your child is never not there, that the option of holding it back is not available, and that closing yourself off to that powerful feeling is not possible, even if you tried.

Now there is a huge difference between that love being absent or you simply not feeling it at the moment, and since it is never absent we don't have to solve a missing case here—meaning no desperate searching, no uptight creating, and certainly no guilting yourself into a lower frequency of "Where is it and what is wrong with me?" is ever needed.

So let's jump right into what is really happening when you can't feel that love.

You are not in an open and receiving mode in which you allow yourself to feel that grand love. That's it!

There are many reasons for the why, but looking deep into the why is not - or at least not always - going to resolve anything, and might even create more unwell feelings. A more helpful practice is to acknowledge the simplicity of "I am not open enough to feel it right now, nothing is wrong, and all is good!"

From there, you shift to accept, respect, appreciate, thank, and love this time as the gift it represents for you—to practice opening yourself up infinitely in order to feel this grand love; to grow into, and with that love; to become one with that love and dance harmoniously with it; and to pack up your whole existence and move into being and living in this love—together with your children.

So what is this "parenthood love cycle" all about?

At the beginning of parenthood, starting all the way back when you make the choice - or not - to be a parent, you hit the red "Let's Go" button that is labeled "Initiate!" and right then, you launch the rocket of this infinite love.

Then, while you are busy giving birth, your sneaky child - or rather their soul being - takes over the lead of that initiated love. And before you know what happened, your whole being is taken over by this wonderful feeling that has now blossomed into the greatest power there is. Think about it, your beginner love is being injected and spiced-up by unlimited vividness through your child.

Next comes what we all know. You and your children grow and grow - sometimes consciously and other times subconsciously - this love to be bigger and bigger over a lifetime together.

"Help me, spend time with me, cook for me, laugh with me, play with me, and love me—with and through that initiated parent love! Also, Mom and Dad, BE that love for yourself!"

~ Your Child

Every age and phase with your children is an important growth factor of said love and of your capability to love as that grand love—nourishing your being and your child's being in the exact spot where nourishment is needed. This shows itself by you feeling loved, needed, valued, confirmed, and purposeful, but not because your children behave a certain way—rather because you ARE that grand love and ARE loving - yourself and your children - as that.

It's all about you and your grand love—not about the inclusion of the child!

We are going to bounce ahead here, because it's very simple through all these years of baby-hood, toddler-hood, and childhood—you grow and grow this grand love together with your child through vivid experiences, and through cuteness, playfulness, joy, and many tearful times.

Then they become tweeners and teenagers!

Suddenly they stop doing all these cute things - with you, to you, or for you - that helped you grow your love in such an easy way. It's like they rip the love-creating-carpet right out from under your feet—leaving you with nothing to stand on anymore.

Right there it hits you! You are all alone in this love quest. You feel lost, are in disbelief, and might even feel resentful or think that they are mean—that they owe you that love.

You ask:

- How could they be so harsh?

- Why did they do that?

- Don't they know who I am? I am their mother/father!

- And who is always there for them?

"Let me break the raw news to you! This is how it is supposed to be! I can't be your love-growing-servant forever!"

~ *Your Child*

Let's get real here!

Think of an adult person who never wants to be done with school and never wants to move out. You would say to them "It's time to be done with school and start a new chapter in your life. You learned all you could in that school, your studying there is finished—your further learning is in life as it happens, after the school years. Go for it, find your dream job and your own wonderful place to live. You got this, you are prepared, you are ready!"

That is exactly what your precious teenagers are signaling to you by rebelling—they are giving you their respect by showing you that you can love on your own now. Their revolt is a huge sign - to make sure you really see it - saying:

"Mom, Dad, it's time for you to graduate from the Love-Growing-University of your children! You went for many, many years, you learned enough, and you know what to do now."

You came into this life just like your children, to take over the lead in initiating and growing the grand love of your parents, while also growing your own love as a child who is turning into an adult—the being that you are now. Then your children arrive, as your initiators and teachers of your infinite parent love until they are teenagers—the right time for them to kick you out of their love university. Actually, the university is closing for good because it ran out of eligible students—you!

You are well beyond graduating and more than ready to go out in the real world to keep growing, nourishing, and multiplying your grand love that you possess, into whatever you want it to be for you.

"I love teaching you how to grow your love—over and over, and most of the time I am very patient. With the high hopes that you are getting it, will have learned it at some point, and then go do it for yourself."

~ *Your Child*

So instead of focusing on them not teaching you anymore - like an angry college student who is mad at the college - turn this incredible opportunity into the best thing that ever happened to you, and for you, by shifting your grand love towards yourself.

"This whole time you thought it was all about you loving me, when all along it was always about you loving yourself. Because of this misconception, you were willing to go all out for that love, for me."

~ *Your Child*

From the beginning it was always only about you!

You going through all these transitions as a parent had nothing to do with your children, and you growing this love into humongous-ness had nothing to do with your children. It was always and only about you—for that when it's time to graduate you can love yourself with confidence in that unconditional humongous way. Your soul-ful way!

Your kids trick you into thinking it was about them, because if you would have known it's for yourself, you would never have put in all this focus in growing this love so infinitely. Instead you would have said, "I am too busy, too tired, and anyways…"

The phase of when your children turn into "monsters," IS nothing else than your children's becoming and also your own becoming. These phases go hand in hand. Your training is over, you are clearly ready, time for those gloriously-mean teenagers to give you a nice and hard nudge—to turn inward and love yourself with - and through - the grandest love there is, and love yourself like you never loved yourself before. A self-love that IS your birthright!

They help you to grow your grand love and then they ask you

to shift it towards yourself! How phenomenally self-less of them and infinitely worthy of a medal is that?

So, not only do you have the right love degree and love diploma, you actually own this grand love. You ARE this grand love!

"You have no more excuses to not love yourself, because the whole word knows that you are highly trained and that you can! Yes, I am a very selfish self-lover and I wish for you to follow my lead to BE and live your love for yourself in the highest form too. Come BE selfish with me!"

~ *Your Child*

You have been tricked by life and by your kids! How lollipop-ish is that?

"Happy Graduation Day Mom and Dad! Life is a peach, isn't it?"

~ *Your Child*

This IS Parenting Through the Eyes of Lollipops!

SOME LOOSE ENDS

In this chapter we will look into different scenarios, talk about snippets of knowledge, and come up with fresh new ways and thoughts to give your parenting experience a new spin into joy.

HAVE A HEALTHY ENVIRONMENT IN EACH COMPONENT

You are a whole being—a physical body, a mind, a soul, and a consciousness. So are your children.

Creating a healthy environment in all of your being IS of utmost importance in order to be able to *Parent Through The Eyes of Lollipops*. Think of being exhausted or unhealthy and trying to see life as sweet and colorful—possible, yet a hard starting point. Feeling well means you can co-create soul-fully by dancing a harmonious dance with your children. Fun times indeed!

So take care of all your components, including:

Your physical body, which has very specific needs at different times and phases in your physical life. To find out what they are, have conversations with your body and ask what it needs—chat with your pain, your physical symptoms, and your physical disharmonies. Follow the answers and instructions with determination and your deepest self-love. Some obvious needs are lots of sleep, plenty of water, fitting movement, and clean food for nourishment; some higher frequency ones are hobbies, meditation, massages, laughter, gratitude, appreciation, and humor—for me, chocolate and wine are definitely high-for-life qualities.

Show your children what it means to take excellent care of a physical body! Encourage them to do the same.

Your mind, which is capable of wonderful thoughts. Acknowledge all of your thoughts as neutral—none are good, none are bad, they just are. Stay judgement free! Accept, respect, appreciate, thank, and love all your incredible thinking as part of you. Then notice the thoughts that are not aiding you and don't make you feel good, shift them to better feeling ones. For instance, from "not enough" to "plenty and abundant" or from "ugly" to "beautiful." Practicing this often makes positive thinking your normal way of living.

Teach your children to embrace all their thoughts too and help them shift to better feeling ones, without judging them or their thoughts.

Your Soul, which is the truth of who you really are—an energetic essence with limitless soul-wisdom you can draw from. Your heart hosts your soul, so it only makes sense to focus on nourishing your heart through creating and experiencing heart-touching moments to fulfill your heart and soul. Consciously feeling these happy times, fills every single cell of your whole being with infinite well-being—happiness guaranteed.

Support your children in the creation of happy moments by smiling and laughing, by dancing and jumping - on your couch or trampoline - or by indulging in treats and giggles. Are you having a laugh at this too? Your children are way ahead in this and teach you at a higher joy department level—follow them and latch onto their natural super-power of having fun.

Make heart-soul nourishment a daily priority!

Your consciousness, your NOW! Focus on what is going right for you in your NOW. This can be your breath giving you life, your feet running after your kids, your job bringing you money, your loved ones, the sun and moon showing up, or anything that is going right for you. If needed, use the help of a mental microscope to find the smallest going-right-particle, because good is always there for you.

Raise your children's consciousnesses into a high-for-life experience by constantly remarking on what is going right for them right now, and by mentioning to them what is going right for you, right now.

Stop talking about what is going wrong! That stops the focus and momentum of the unwanted, giving the wanted a chance to BE. Instead say, "It always works out for me, for you, and for us!" which supports your children in being and living with a positive attitude.

Creating a healthy environment in all of your being's components - body, mind, soul, consciousness - is an inspiring demonstration of well-being for your children. It offers a solid foundation for them, especially when they get tested in their own unique ways during the teenage years and beyond.

It is never too late for you or your children to start being positive, healthy, and happy - while remaining to BE your soul being - and to make it your normal way of living this physical life. However, the earlier you start, the better.

Keep in mind that the change in the job taking and filling for who the spiritual and who the physical teachers or students are is a constant one, so be on alert Mom and Dad.

Your children are speedsters!

If trouble arises, stop and ask yourself honestly:

"Am I filling the right job right now?"

"Am I studying the right subject right now?"

"Is my child teaching me physically or spiritually right now?"

"Am I dancing a harmonious dance with my child?"

To harmonize, quit the unfitting job that you are holding on for dear life, and with your deepest gratitude, go fill the right and fitting one for right now. No harm done, just a bit of clarity needed and a wonderful adjustment accomplished!

This IS Parenting Through the Eyes of Lollipops!

LIVE PRESSURE-FREE

"Pressure turns me into mashed potatoes—too mushy to think!

~ *Your Child*

Have you ever watched or used a pressure cooker? Then you know the power it has, to change whatever is cooking in no time. The energy present in there also has the potential to be powerfully harmful when opened to peek while it is cooking— dangerous and threatening. It does warn us to use with caution!

Pressure in life has the same effect for you and your children. Pressure threatens, endangers, and can powerfully harm the well-being of the ones involved. Pressure changes you, changes your children, and it changes the output in physical life—in no time. Use with caution!

Pressuring someone means:

- A lack of trust in oneself to follow one's own soul-calling of being and living happily—no matter the circumstances. If full trust is present, pressuring someone to change for anyone else is out of the equation.

- A lack of trust in a person's ability to follow their own unique soul-calling to be and live happily—no matter the circumstances. If complete trust is there, the knowledge that they have everything in them is absolute, making pressuring them a non-existing entity.

Working on your trust when pressuring another person is definitely the key to unlocking the door to pressure-free co-creation!

However, pressure can also be based on unfitting expectations—dramatically spoken, expectations are like fiery rockets that might or might not hit the target. If it's a hit, it's a party! If it's a miss, the destruction can be devastating.

To neutralize the strong energy of pressure, let go of all expectations of how you, your children, parenthood, family time, and really anything has to BE. Allow the creative life-style of realizing that everyone and everything exists in many different ways, colors, moods, shapes, sizes, forms, feelings, needs, and desires.

Feel the opportunities for magnificence when you let go of the expectation that your child has to behave a certain way and trust in your child's ability to follow its own soul-calling. Your encounter will be one of soul-to-soul that is based on love and trust. All solutions that fit both of you reside on such wonderful ground.

To take it further...

When you let go of expectations and acknowledge that everything just IS - nothing good, nothing bad - even a screaming bloody-murder noise will shift to be pressure-free.

From your newfound space of thinking that it IS what it IS, you can then nourish your trust by following your own soul-calling and experience everyone and everything through your pressure-free way of being and living as your relaxed YOU.

Keep in mind that the change in the job taking and filling for who the spiritual and who the physical teachers or students are is a constant one, so be on alert Mom and Dad.

Your children are speedsters!

If trouble arises, stop and ask yourself honestly:

"Am I filling the right job right now?"

"Am I studying the right subject right now?"

"Is my child teaching me physically or spiritually right now?"

"Am I dancing a harmonious dance with my child?"

To harmonize, quit the unfitting job that you are holding on for dear life, and with your deepest gratitude, go fill the right and fitting one for right now. No harm done, just a bit of clarity needed and a wonderful adjustment accomplished!

This IS Parenting Through the Eyes of Lollipops!

LIVE RESISTANCE-FREE

"Mom, Dad, resistance can be like roadblocks that we have to jump over in order to keep dancing in harmony together—not smooth moves at all!"

~ Your Child

Resistance in children surfaces naturally when they are made to do something that does not fit for them—this type of resisting is not a hold-back since it originates from their soul-calling saying, "It does not feel good so I don't want to do it!"

If their resistance is not freely chosen by them, but rather taught - and not explained to them - by others, it becomes an unfitting copied belief for the child. This can be a hindrance, because if they don't feel or know why they are resisting, how can it truly empower their soul being? In this scenario, resistance is a possible set back in life, because if what we resist is something that we want, it cannot be received. What if the child would want what they were taught to resist? And if the taught resistance highlights something that we don't want, the unwanted gets stronger in energy because of the momentum that our resistance carries—meaning that fighting something puts enormous focus on the unwanted, creating our next unwanted experience. A hold-back!

"You keep playing your old resistances like a bad old movie—renewing them all the time! Take a break, breathe, and dance with me in my resistance-free wildness!"

~ Your Child

Resistance in parents originates mostly from old resistance-beliefs that are replayed over and over, and from expectations that are falsely set for yourselves and others—to recap, expectations are the equivalent of setting off fiery rockets that might or might not hit the target, making wrongful destruction a real possibility.

"By resisting, I train and show off my superhero strength, a soul-power that I already AM and will need to BE in my journey. When you see my resistant warrior surfacing, celebrate it with me!"

~ *Your Child*

Celebrating? What?

"But what about brushing teeth, or eating the right food?" you might ask.

When children receive full trust of the parents, have the freedom to choose, and are educated about their choices, they usually want to - and actually do - choose well for themselves— even if the choice is not the best, they learn a great deal by choosing for themselves. In that freedom, resistance has no space because it is their free will.

In contrast, children made to do something that does not fit for them resist strongly—but on a positive note, it is a great showcase of how strong and powerful they really are!

"I want to thank you for giving me all these opportunities to practice, show off, and grow my resistance strength—without you this power of mine would be dormant and not known. You testing my resistance gives me confidence. Thank you!"

~ *Your Child*

Depending on your choice of parenting, either give them the freedom to choose or celebrate their phenomenal will and power of resistance. Both of these scenarios are great opportunities to **Parent Through The Eyes of Lollipops**—soul to soul.

Certainly never punish them for their resistance, because you are punishing them for being their soul being and following their soul-calling.

"Know that what I resist does not fit for me because something about it is not my truth. Do you really want me to BE anything else but my truth?"

~ *Your Child*

Let them learn on their own terms. Let them find their way. Let them BE. Most of all, learn from them to go for your own freedom too and to choose fittingly for you—removing the need to resist so much in your life because more and more of it will be from your free will.

To live resistance-free means that you change your old beliefs into new and more fitting ones, letting go of all those silly expectations. Here is how:

- Acknowledge everyone and everything as IS without judging

- Accept, respect, appreciate, thank, and love everyone and everything as IS

Your child is clearly your spiritual teacher here, teaching you how to let go of your old non-fitting beliefs, how to be more in line with your truth, and how to write a whole new story about your resistance-free life. For balance, you are the physical teacher, teaching them about physical life chores that they resist—helping your children grow their power of staying in alignment with their soul-truth. Plus, you help them train the voices of their choices to be loud and clear.

"Don't you love how resistance shifts from negative to a beautiful thing that we get to practice together?"

~ Your Child

Keep in mind that the change in the job taking and filling for who the spiritual and who the physical teachers or students are is a constant one, so be on alert Mom and Dad.

Your children are speedsters!

If trouble arises, stop and ask yourself honestly:

"Am I filling the right job right now?"

"Am I studying the right subject right now?"

"Is my child teaching me physically or spiritually right now?"

"Am I dancing a harmonious dance with my child?"

To harmonize, quit the unfitting job that you are holding on for dear life, and with your deepest gratitude, go fill the right and fitting one for right now. No harm done, just a bit of clarity needed and a wonderful adjustment accomplished!

This IS Parenting Through the Eyes of Lollipops!

HAPPINESS

"Happiness is not something you do, it IS something that you ARE!"

~ Jacqueline Pirtle

When you do happiness it is exhausting, because you rely on happy feelings from outside your soul being and from physical-life things, people, and experiences that are in your awareness. In this scenario, you must be a speed runner by now—constantly running around searching for things to feel good. The story goes on... once you find your object of happiness, you don't even have the time to really milk that well-feeling, because hey, these items are many times very short lived and most people don't stay behaved long enough for you to catch a breath in that good feeling.

But can you really blame them when the natural essence of physical life IS ever-changing, ever-vibrating, ever-renewing, and ever-refreshing in every split second there IS? When every breath you take is new, every step you take is new, every split second you are experiencing is new?

This type of happiness also highlights all the worries and pressure that are created by latching your happiness onto what's out there—hence opinions and questions like, "Will they behave so I can be happy?" or "What if there is nothing to be happy about?" and "What if it does not last?" which is not a happy way to BE happy at all!

The best way to experience happiness is when you consciously tune into the fact that you ARE happiness and that happiness IS you. Yes, you are a walking energetic being - a soul being - made of pure positive energy! Happiness, well-being, joy, love, and all positivity are the perfect energetic match to who you really are; your truthful being. That is why feeling good feels so good—there is no split energy present, in you, or for you.

Happiness IS always with you, as you—you two are never separate. It's the best package deal ever!

Let me explain…

- Your physical body, making this physical life experience possible—That IS happiness!

- Your mind, able to think - positive - thoughts—That IS happiness!

- Your soul, the energetic you that IS pure positive energy—That IS happiness!

- Your consciousness, your NOW that is always treating you with something good—That IS happiness!

- Your breath giving you the means to live—That IS happiness!

- Your blood pumping the energy to BE—That IS happiness!

- Your smile shifting anything into joy—That IS happiness!

- Your feet carrying you miles and miles—That IS happiness!

- You, who ARE an energetic being having this physical life experience—That IS happiness!

Basing your well-feeling on the happiness that you ARE means that no matter the

circumstances you can feel good, you can smile, you can choose joy, and you can BE happy and fill yourself to the brim with that guaranteed well-feeling. Plus, you get to recycle all the goodness that you manifested - by simply being your own happiness - through experiencing it all deliberately—because how you feel right now creates your next, fills your happy tank to the brim and into overflow, and shares and spreads well-being to everyone and everything.

The way to teach and share this happiness knowledge with your children is by being your happiness as deliberately, and as consciously as often as you can—they will catch on to this with speed. Then again, who are we kidding here...

Your still pure children are much better at naturally and automatically being their own happinesses. Why not give in, and let yourself be led by the best of the best at all times? Led by your happy kids?

Keep in mind that the change in the job taking and filling for who the spiritual and who the physical teachers or students are is a constant one, so be on alert Mom and Dad.

Your children are speedsters!

If trouble arises, stop and ask yourself honestly:

"Am I filling the right job right now?"

"Am I studying the right subject right now?"

"Is my child teaching me physically or spiritually right now?"

"Am I dancing a harmonious dance with my child?"

To harmonize, quit the unfitting job that you are holding on for dear life, and with your deepest gratitude, go fill the right and fitting one for right now. No harm done, just a bit of clarity needed and a wonderful adjustment accomplished!

For a deeper understanding and more happiness practice pick up my bestselling book *365 Days of Happiness: Because happiness is a piece of cake*. Available as a paperback, kindle, mobile app, along with a companion self-study program that fortifies the teachings. *365 Days of Happiness* compliments *Parenting Through the Eyes of Lollipops*—they go hand in hand in learning to BE and live happier lives as a whole.

This IS Parenting Through the Eyes of Lollipops!

LIVING FROM MY HEART

"Your heart is the home of your soul - your deepest inner being, your absolute knowing, and your true space of belonging - besides being a love-feeling factory for you."

~ Your Child

As parents, you have the ability to multiply an unlimited love that is being unleashed in you at high-speed—a love that is always available for you to shower your children with.

Living from your heart means living from a foundation of that love—of "it feels right," of kindness, playfulness, joy, fulfillment, happiness, well-being, and well-feeling.

So why is it that we don't use this love-creating mechanism at all times?

The culprit is a disconnection, an un-belonging, or a lack of knowing. When you catch yourself not living from that sweet spot, you are not the soul essence that IS you. You might not know that you ARE a soul, maybe you are not aware that you have a soul-home or where it is, or have no idea how to get there—maybe never even got the chance to practice being your soul, living in your soul-home.

It's simple, you are not home!

That homeless feeling rattles up all sorts of insecurities, especially in times when your truth is shown to you in ways that go deeply against the parent superhero that you so much want to be.

"What my heart tells me to do, say, want, feel, or think might not always fit with what you are wanting it to. That is okay, because my heart is different than yours. Be wise as to what fights you want to take up against my heart, because it's pretty strong—combine that with my wise soul being and even sturdier mind... And I let you draw your own conclusions."

~ Your Child

The fix for this type of homelessness is to go home, not to change your children. It's an opportunity for you to occupy your heart, your soul, who you really are, and to not leave for any amount of time just to be homeless again. In your soul being, you are always that superhero—for you! Feeling this is a phenomenal shift of focus onto yourself and the huge love-creator that you are—no matter the circumstances.

Commit, practice, and grow a passion to feel what it means for you to BE and live in your home—a place from where you can experience love, joy, well-being, well-feeling, and pure happiness.

A great exercise for becoming a home-staying master is to consciously feel all the cute moments, play-times, fun talks, and giggles with your younger children and notice the well-feeling that your older children are experiencing—latch on to these wonderful ways of home-being.

Don't choose - yes, it's your choice - to leave your home just because there is a rough patch on the horizon. Stay in your heart space and BE yourself from there! Your well-feeling will catch your children's subconscious attention, showing them how they can BE and live their truth too.

…Keep reading, as the following chapter Feeling Good As The Highest Priority! continues this heart-felt conversation.

Keep in mind that the change in the job taking and filling for who the spiritual and who the physical teachers or students are is a constant one, so be on alert Mom and Dad.

Your children are speedsters!

If trouble arises, stop and ask yourself honestly:

"Am I filling the right job right now?"

"Am I studying the right subject right now?"

"Is my child teaching me physically or spiritually right now?"

"Am I dancing a harmonious dance with my child?"

To harmonize, quit the unfitting job that you are holding on for dear life, and with your deepest gratitude, go fill the right and fitting one for right now. No harm done, just a bit of clarity needed and a wonderful adjustment accomplished!

This IS Parenting Through the Eyes of Lollipops!

FEELING GOOD AS MY HIGHEST PRIORITY

"Feeling good is my imprinted way of being! Let's be honest, I can't stand laying in a dirty diaper because it does not feel good—it's itchy and it burns. So I cry my lungs out to get you to change my diaper, right now, so I can feel good again ASAP!"

~ *Your Child*

Let's see how feeling good really feels:

Imagine that you are traveling deep into your heart—the factory of your love and the home of your soul. On this journey, you go through many layers of different feelings until you feel so high-for-life that you know with sureness that you have arrived, because everything...

...looks like through the eyes of lollipops; colorful, fun, happy

...feels like through the emotions of lollipops; playful, joyful, well

...sounds like through the ears of lollipops; musical, harmonious

...tastes like through the mouth of lollipops; sweet, delicious

...smells like thorough the nose of lollipops; let's just say candy-lishious

...thinks like through the mind of lollipops; positive, hopeful, grateful

You are so in awe there and like it so much that you decide to sign a lease for life, grab all your belongings, move in, and stay in your good feeling heart forever and ever.

Isn't that what you want for your children too?

Their heart is that place where they can live free to act, say, think, feel, do, decide, and learn—to make good choices, be kind, happy, and healthy, and where they can feel good.

Your children want this, actually, it's their highest priority!

Every time they don't feel good, they demand to do or have something to make them feel good again, or feel better—which explains why simply saying "no" to them won't work, because in reality you are saying to your child "No, you can't feel better. You cannot live in your heart. I won't allow it!"

"Realize that my tantrums - be it kid-sized or young-adult-sized - are all about me wanting to feel better!"

~ *Your Child*

A lot of the time parents experience the child's constant wanting more through their own old beliefs of "they are never grateful," or "they are greedy," or "they are never satisfied because it's never enough." But is that really true?

Wanting to feel good or always a little better is a phenomenal natural instinct, an automatic knowing, and everyone's true soul-calling. Feeling good is a physical-life-match to your soul being and the pure positive energy that you are. So no, the above is completely untrue!

"It is of utmost importance to me to feel good! In truth, it's the same for you, Mom and Dad!"

~ *Your Child*

I am not suggesting that you always give in or always have to make your child's wishes come true - because some are best when realized through their own doing - but it's something to consider and worth trying to achieve, also for your own wishes.

It's the understanding that really counts here, that you understand that:

• Your child is wired to always want to feel good or feel better. It's their soul's calling!

- You are wired like that too, but have un-learned it. So get back at it!

- It has nothing to do with you when they want more or better —it's only about them

Your negative thoughts and feelings about them wanting more and better are yours to feel, carry, cleanse, and throw out the window—they are your old beliefs and don't aid you, let alone help you. So what new beliefs can make you feel better?

Just for sanity's sake, imagine what a lack of wanting to feel better would do to this physical world. It would be a boring, dead-end world—might as well just call it a day and go back to the non-physical.

There is a lot of physical teaching opportunity for you to show your children what is possible right now in this physical life —what funds are available right now. Spiritually, on the other hand, your children are showing you clearly that feeling good is your birthright, your soul-calling, why you are here on earth, and worth every tantrum in the world.

"I say follow the leader—me!"

~ Your Child

Keep in mind that the change in the job taking and filling for who the spiritual and who the physical teachers or students are is a constant one, so be on alert Mom and Dad.

Your children are speedsters!

If trouble arises, stop and ask yourself honestly:

"Am I filling the right job right now?"

"Am I studying the right subject right now?"

"Is my child teaching me physically or spiritually right now?"

"Am I dancing a harmonious dance with my child?"

To harmonize, quit the unfitting job that you are holding on for dear life, and with your deepest gratitude, go fill the right and fitting one for right now. No harm done, just a bit of clarity needed and a wonderful adjustment accomplished!

This IS Parenting Through the Eyes of Lollipops!

PASSION

"Passion never has to make sense!"

~ Your Child

Passion is created by following your soul calling without any other reason other than feeling wonderful and losing yourself in that calling. It is a direct nutritional injection into your soul being that feeds who you really are.

When passion is lived, it creates happiness, harmony, balance, and a more expanded soul being. Since the truest part in everyone is their soul-being, wouldn't it be a given that you want yours and those of your children to be humongous? Letting passion rule means you accomplish exactly that.

Your children are pure, clean, fresh, and new in their physical essence—they will do things without finding reasons, then lose themselves in that freedom, growing their soul-passions and expanding more into who they really are. How much more soul-passionate can it get?

If you interrupt them by asking too many why's, what's, how's, and who's, they will start to think about their passions, shifting them to act on more physical-life-passions—versus feeling pure soul-passions that are true soul-callings. Plus, there is a huge possibility that they don't even know the why because children naturally operate from the automatic knowing on their soul-level. Let's not mess with that—instead commit to leave them be.

You have the option to be a great copycat by following your children's lead to lose yourself in your freedom too. Join in! Sing with your children when doing dishes, draw with them before going to bed, write in a happiness journal while sitting with your children, play when they are playing. Incorporate everything that feels wonderful into your time, both with them and without them

—growing your passions and expanding your soul being into humongous-ness. NOW you are Parenting Through the Eyes of Lollipops—the eyes of your soul being!

Treat passions as the highest form of well-being, and know that every person who is lost in their passion is actually very "found" in feeding their soul into a humongous expansion. If your children are happy while doing something, they are growing their passion by following their soul-knowing—end of story. If watching them and feeling their happiness, their presence, and their essence beats your drum of well-feeling, go for it! Enjoy, learn, and embrace this simple pleasure called passion that feeds your soul while watching magic unfold.

Keep in mind that the change in the job taking and filling for who the spiritual and who the physical teachers or students are is a constant one, so be on alert Mom and Dad.

Your children are speedsters!

If trouble arises, stop and ask yourself honestly:

"Am I filling the right job right now?"

"Am I studying the right subject right now?"

"Is my child teaching me physically or spiritually right now?"

"Am I dancing a harmonious dance with my child?"

To harmonize, quit the unfitting job that you are holding on for dear life, and with your deepest gratitude, go fill the right and fitting one for right now. No harm done, just a bit of clarity needed and a wonderful adjustment accomplished!

This IS Parenting Through the Eyes of Lollipops!

HUMOR

"Mom, Dad, my biggest interest is fun, play, and to feel good and smile—especially when little. I AM that way! That's the way I learn, grow, expand, and how I create my personality—and in all honesty, so do you!"

~ Your Young Child

Your humor will carry you to solutions you never really thought of, because in a space of humor you relax and naturally open up to allow soul-ful ideas to present themselves—letting you choose resolutions that feel good for you and your children.

Think of it this way:

Humor carries the energy of being care-free, fun, playful, having an easy come easy go mentality, creativity, and childlikeness. When you are indulging in humor you shift to BE and live in those "where all the fun resides" frequencies—shifting everyone and everything - except teenagers and people that are not willing - to BE and live there too by sharing and spreading your fun energy.

*"**Parenting Through the Eyes of Lollipops** means:*

When I am grumpy, BE that lollipop for me!

When I am tired, BE that lollipop for me!

When I am mean, BE that lollipop for me!

When I am unfair, BE that lollipop for me!

When I am hangry, BE that lollipop for me!

When I am a wild rebel child, BE that lollipop for me!

All other joyous times, I AM the lollipop for you!

That evens it out, doesn't it? I lollipop - love - you forever!"

~ Your Child

Teenagers have to be met where they are—not that you have to match their anger, but you need to find common ground, and humor is not always the solution. In other words:

Imagine that your teenager is eating ice cream and you are eating garlic—you are trying to make the case that there is a common ground between garlic and ice cream. Your teenager will look at you like you are crazy and not buy into that, because there really is no common ground between ice cream and garlic. At least, not until you magically whip out a carton of garlic ice cream out of the freezer, showing that to your teenager. Suddenly the conversation is not about garlic or ice cream anymore, it's about garlic ice cream, meaning that you found common ground. And yes, there is such a thing as garlic ice cream!

"P.S. When I am eating ice cream, don't BE the garlic for me!"

~ Your Teenager

Keep in mind that the change in the job taking and filling for who the spiritual and who the physical teachers or students are is a constant one, so be on alert Mom and Dad.

Your children are speedsters!

If trouble arises, stop and ask yourself honestly:

"Am I filling the right job right now?"

"Am I studying the right subject right now?"

"Is my child teaching me physically or spiritually right now?"

"Am I dancing a harmonious dance with my child?"

To harmonize, quit the unfitting job that you are holding on for dear life, and with your deepest gratitude, go fill the right and fitting one for right now. No harm done, just a bit of clarity needed and a wonderful adjustment accomplished!

This IS Parenting Through the Eyes of Lollipops!

BIG WISHES AND EVEN BIGGER DREAMS

"I want nothing more than for me to be your biggest dream and wish forever!!! However, I understand that this would limit you and limit me. So let's just agree that you keep me as your biggest dream for as long as you can - which should not be for that long - and then, with speed, please go and dream on—beyond me."

~ Your Child

Let's get straight into **Parenting Through the Eyes of Lollipops** with this one!

"I am clearly your spiritual teacher in this, at least at first, because having a baby lifts every parent's bar of wishes and dreams of what actually IS possible."

~ Your Child

Big wishes and dreams are the fuel that turns desires into a happy life creation! It is fact that physical life is created by what and how you think, see, hear, taste, smell, and feel right now. Meaning, if you are positive, you create your next experience in your life as a positive one—same goes for being negative; it builds and creates forward and onward.

Here is another way of looking at it:

Imagine that you are laying out the tiles for the path in your physical journey, tile by tile. While standing on a tile right now you lay your next forward tile for you to stand on. If you are standing on a happy tile, you just laid your next happy tile. If you are standing on an unhappy one, to avoid laying the next unhappy one, you have to put all your forces into gear and shift to happiness, laying your next happy tile.

"I want you to wish and dream big! Nope, you are not there there yet… Go even bigger!"

~ Your Child

Walk your physical life journey while being and living those big dreams, wishes, and goals of yours. Become them! Feel one with them! That is how life knows what tiles you are laying for yourself—your soul has your back and the universe is always listening and always delivering!

The bigger you wish and the more you wish for, the better of an idol you are for your children—and the more inspired they get to do the same. The more you let your children be and stay the big wishers and dreamers that they came to be in this physical life, the more you will remember that you started out this way too.

"The more you do this high-for-life wishing and dreaming for you, the more you will allow me to do it for me."

~ *Your Child*

Feel the "uplifting each other" and the "higher and higher" energies with each other that is created by bouncing your wishes and dreams off of one another—setting the happiness bar higher and higher. Happy souls guaranteed!

And to whoever might say "too big, too much, not possible," send them your biggest smile and know that they have forgotten who they really are. Who knows, you might end up being the inspiration that they needed to remember.

BE dream-partners and wish-partners with your children!

Create castles with them!

Never ever believe in any limits!

Keep in mind that the change in the job taking and filling for who the spiritual and who the physical teachers or students are is a constant one, so be on alert Mom and Dad.

Your children are speedsters!

If trouble arises, stop and ask yourself honestly:

"Am I filling the right job right now?"

"Am I studying the right subject right now?"

"Is my child teaching me physically or spiritually right now?"

"Am I dancing a harmonious dance with my child?"

To harmonize, quit the unfitting job that you are holding on for dear life, and with your deepest gratitude, go fill the right and fitting one for right now. No harm done, just a bit of clarity needed and a wonderful adjustment accomplished!

This IS Parenting Through the Eyes of Lollipops!

WHO IS WHAT ENERGY IN THE FAMILY?

Imagine that every family member is a certain energy. The different energies are:

Water: Denser in movement, peaceful, harmonious

Earth: Mountainous, strong, unshakable

Fire: Fiery, moving fast, shaking things up

Air: Basing everything on fun and light-ness

Each family member is made out of all of the above energies, yet one is always dominant per person—either water, earth, fire, or air. Whatever dominant energy one is carrying is the energetic value said person is best capable of offering and teaching to the whole family.

Together, this family has the potential to experience a co-creation that is soul-fully complete and balanced—meaning the energetic value of that whole family is healthy and happy, because every family member brings a profound value to life. In that wholesome entity, everyone is cherished and appreciated.

Finding out the energy of each member of your family and understanding their individual energetic value - what they can offer and teach - shifts everyone, no matter how different, to be an important part of the family.

This also invites you to look at their gifts and refuse to focus on what looks like limits or holdbacks—which, on a soul level, are never real and true anyways.

But stay alert! Dominant energies can change rapidly through the expansion and evolution of a person - through life experiences - so re-evaluate often!

Let's say you have a denser moving and deeper feeling person in the family. That person helps to keep the family deeply grounded and living at a slower pace—a wonderful energy to have present since family life is a very fast-paced time. Celebrate their energetic value and the peace and rest they bring, and the constant reminder of peaceful sanity. They are like saints.

If you have a fast-paced person in the family who likes to "stay on the surface," realize that their energetic value is all about keeping everyone - especially the parents - on their toes by creating a speedy evolution and expansion while also teaching that it is okay to stay "on the surface" about physical life things, and not fall to deeply into unwell feelings—not every physical life happening needs to be dissected. They are movers and shakers!

Say you have a strong, steady, and grounding force in the family. They keep it all together like a mountain, and are mostly focused on the physical aspect of life. Welcome that energy to keep the whole family grounded and in a safe feeling. Lean on them, they love that!

And then there is that light, bubbly, and mostly high-for-life wild energetic being. They are either all the way high up or all the way down low—with the ability to bounce around in split seconds. They base everything on having fun and being happy— embrace their bubbly values, even if they are annoying, when you are on the heavier side. They are the sunshine at all times!

Every family member, even the pets, have an energetic value that they bring forth to make your family whole. Everyone is infinitely valuable, everyone has something to teach, and everyone has something to learn—which brings about phenomenal co-creation from soul-to-soul.

Keep in mind that the change in the job taking and filling for who the spiritual and who the physical teachers or students are is a constant one, so be on alert Mom and Dad.

Your children are speedsters!

If trouble arises, stop and ask yourself honestly:

"Am I filling the right job right now?"

"Am I studying the right subject right now?"

"Is my child teaching me physically or spiritually right now?"

"Am I dancing a harmonious dance with my child?"

To harmonize, quit the unfitting job that you are holding on for dear life, and with your deepest gratitude, go fill the right and fitting one for right now. No harm done, just a bit of clarity needed and a wonderful adjustment accomplished!

This IS Parenting Through the Eyes of Lollipops!

SICK CHILDREN

Naturally, you give everything that you have when your children don't feel well—even if it means you are running yourself into the ground or running beyond empty. At first glance, this looks like a labor of love; however, it's not. It's a labor of fear - especially when it involves your children - meaning that somewhere in this you shifted from serving through pure love, keeping yourself afloat, to serving through something like a fear of "I have to give it all I got, or else…"

When you are empty, or run down, it is a clear sign that you are not dipping into the infinite pool of your soul essence and soul wisdom - your energetic resources - to experience life, instead living mostly through and as your physical being—which has limits. In case you think a mix might work… not really! Serving from split energy - a mix of love and fear - still means that you are not feeling the "well-est" while taking care of your sick child.

Serving from pure love - your soul being - means you are doing everything that you can for your child, in health and in sickness, without ever running empty—because when you serve from you soul being there is never a limit as to how much love and care you can give. A soul has no bottom, and never will reach the bottom of pure energy that is available for you to utilize.

Why is this so important?

Feeling good is your biggest soul expansion. No soul ever came here to not feel good—being the complete positive energy they are. And just for thought, no soul ever wants to be put into the backseat to do nothing, while having to watch the physical self facepalm their way through life by living old beliefs, by being unhappy, feeling run-down, and not wanting to be here.

Take this to heart, and serve only as and through your pure love—meaning that it feels good to serve. Notice your shift when helping your child does not feel good anymore. Take a break, find your soul place again, and on you go—serving the both of you.

You share your energy with your children at all times. An energy of fear is not something that will help your child to heal or feel better, yet an energy of pure love will do the supportive healing-trick.

"I have my own path as my physical person in this physical life and whatever sickness I am going through is mine to experience. Even if I don't love my sickness - you will be informed of that by my constant crying - and I do not feel good being sick, it is not yours to feel deeply and fully."

~ *Your Child*

Remember, your child has a powerful soul guidance available that knows how to be healthy and is capable of being healthy—just like you. Your pure love is an energetic match to that soul guidance—supporting its power.

Serving, caring for, helping, and nursing your sick child back to health while you are in your soul space means that you separate yourself from the illness of your child and how your child feels—keeping your healing love flowing directly from your soul to your child's soul, the most potent healing method ever!

Practice trust in your child's:

- Soul knowing of how to be healthy

- Soul capability to be healthy

- Physical symptoms to spark a soul "know-how" healing reaction for your child

To support the healing, see, hear, think, talk to and about, and feel your child as completely healthy—no matter the situation. Consciously visualize your absolute knowing of that complete health reaching your child's soul being—filling and replenishing your child with pure well-being. End this practice with your highest gratitude. This is a wonderful energy healing method, no matter the age of your children.

None of the above is medical advice—it is an energy healing approach. Take your child to the doctor if needed, get your children all the help possible and get yourself help too.

Keep in mind that the change in the job taking and filling for who the spiritual and who the physical teachers or students are is a constant one, so be on alert Mom and Dad.

Your children are speedsters!

If trouble arises, stop and ask yourself honestly:

"Am I filling the right job right now?"

"Am I studying the right subject right now?"

"Is my child teaching me physically or spiritually right now?"

"Am I dancing a harmonious dance with my child?"

To harmonize, quit the unfitting job that you are holding on for dear life, and with your deepest gratitude, go fill the right and fitting one for right now. No harm done, just a bit of clarity needed and a wonderful adjustment accomplished!

This IS Parenting Through the Eyes of Lollipops!

ORDERING YOUR CHILD TO HUG AND KISS

"When I refuse to hug, kiss, encounter, or even look at someone, I mean it! That refusal comes from my deep knowing of my truth. It is right and real for me! Letting me say "no" right from the beginning of our time together lets me grow my self-worth-knowing and step into my soul-power."

~ Your Child

Imagine a world with the expectation that the parents do not choose who or what they like, instead putting all their feelings away to obey what they are told to do—to hug and kiss everyone and everything when ordered to do so by their children. This would not be a free environment to BE in.

Obviously, this picture is the other way around in real life. It happens over and over all the time, sometimes with conscious knowing from the parents, and sometimes without parents realizing what they are actually doing when ordering their children to hug and kiss someone, a loved one, or even the parents themselves.

"See me as the soul that I am, not just a physical child! You would never order a soul to do something. And just for giggles... Imagine that I am an old soul. You can't ask an old soul to hug and kiss."

~ Your Child

Mostly this stems from old beliefs, antique programming, and unfitting habits of obeying or making the parent feel better—but it also highlights the non-existing acknowledgement that all children are soul beings with an inner knowing, here to live a physical life that only fits their soul calling.

The "Ordering Your Child To Hug and Kiss" practice is never fitting, never aiding, and never an act of unconditional and pure love, let alone respect—no matter the circumstances, the upbringing, the faith or belief. Instead, it initiates children to turn themselves off by wandering far from their truth and well-being —clearly overstepping on the soul-level!

Parenting Through the Eyes of Lollipops **shifts this to become something more like this:**

Imagine a world where everyone is free to decide - to choose - who and what to hug and kiss, without those choices ever being questioned—because everyone acknowledges that everyone is the same; a free soul being, in charge for all yes's and all no's.

Feel the safe, empowering, respectful, and true feelings that are created in you by reading the above. Now imagine the gracious feelings that children feel when living it.

If unsure, ask the child if you can hug and kiss them—if they want to hug and kiss. This teaches them early on that they are in charge of their whole being, a very soul-empowering upbringing. Children will - if left to choose for themselves - hug and kiss when it is right for them—making any hug and kiss truthful and unconditional. A soul-fully wonderful experience for both the hugger and the one being hugged.

Letting your children say no while being their biggest supporter of their refusal shifts you into being the spiritual student in this situation. As your spiritual teachers, your children are demonstrating you how to stand up for your own soul-choices—maybe you were not very free to speak your no's as a child.

"Letting me BE your spiritual teacher in this, will teach you personal freedom and heal your inner child's wounds of people overstepping your soul being."

~ *Your Child*

For harmony's sake, your child will be your physical student, learning from you how to stand up for themselves in this physical world by witnessing you standing up for them and yourself—by not asking them to hug or kiss someone in the first place and by telling that someone "No! My child does not want to hug and kiss you and they do not have to. So back off!"

"My physical body IS mine.

My choices are mine.

My freedom is mine.

And so is yours! Claim it with me!"

~ Your Child

Keep in mind that the change in the job taking and filling for who the spiritual and who the physical teachers or students are is a constant one, so be on alert Mom and Dad.

Your children are speedsters!

If trouble arises, stop and ask yourself honestly:

"Am I filling the right job right now?"

"Am I studying the right subject right now?"

"Is my child teaching me physically or spiritually right now?"

"Am I dancing a harmonious dance with my child?"

To harmonize, quit the unfitting job that you are holding on for dear life, and with your deepest gratitude, go fill the right and fitting one for right now. No harm done, just a bit of clarity needed and a wonderful adjustment accomplished!

If an encounter is of an abusive nature or of sexual nature, don't look away! It's never okay to cross these boundaries! Do something about it! Respect and protect your children, and the children of other families. Get help for them and get help for yourself.

This IS Parenting Through the Eyes of Lollipops!

FOOD STORIES

"We will never really see eye to eye on food, because I am not you."

~ Your Child

Imagine a world where everyone has the same food needs, and same food cravings; where everyone experiences food the same way, has the same food joys, feels the same way about different types of food, and always want the same foods prepared the same way, at the same time.

I see you are already giggling or rolling your eyes at this. That's okay!

Food and feeding time involving your own children can unleash some strong and intense feelings in parents, showing what we all know—we hit the jackpot with this one!

The good news is, it is an easy-peasy situation to solve. The even better news is that it is all up to you—putting you in charge to shift the subject of food into a harmonious dance with your children. In truth, your old recordings and antique beliefs about food don't fit anymore and most likely never really did. So let's change them.

"I am not a picky eater, I just want to eat what fits my mood - my energy - right now."

~ Your Child

Parenting Through the Eyes of Lollipops shifts this to become this:

Imagine yourself living in a world where, when you desire cake, it arrives in front of your face; when you think salad, it arrives in your bowl; and when you say cheese, cheese fills your watering mouth, giving you a smile. Imagining this food-enhanced world makes you happy because all of your food needs - energetic needs since food is energy - are always met by you, right then and there. What a wonderful way to BE and live with food—with energy.

Food is not just the same old boring nourishment or the fun and yummy intake that some enjoy. Food is energy, vibrating in different frequencies, while carrying different information making some foods - depending on the food and the different needs and likes of various people - a higher frequency than others.

"I might like something sweet, whereas you feel like something salty, or I choose something soft and you like crunchy."

~ *Your Child*

Think about it…

A cucumber initiates a different feeling than a piece of meat, for instance. For some, a cucumber carries the energies of fresh, juicy, green, energizing, and watery, whereas for some it's an energy mix of slimy, earthy, gassy, and yuck. Meat on the other hand carries the energies of hardy, tasty, real food, and packed with power for some, whereas for others it feels simply gross or not the right kind of food.

Take it even further…

For some, meat is a very needed energy, making it a high vibrating energy for them. For others meat is of a very low energy - hard to digest - because they are in need of different energy; vegetables, making the vegetables a high vibrating energy for them.

"Even though we are both the same - souls - we have different needs and desires with what kind of energy we like to fill ourselves with. Sometimes you like to read and I love to play, sometimes I want to go outside and you would rather stay inside. Food is no different."

~ *Your Child*

And let's take it even further…

Some are hungry right now, meaning that if they ate right

now, they energize and use that energy for their physical body to work and to move, their mind to think positive thoughts, their soul to be happy, and their consciousness to be vivid. Eating for them right now is fitting and nourishing in every way.

Others are not hungry right now, meaning that if they would eat because it is dinner time and everyone is eating their food right now, eating is not the energizing and nourishing act that it could be.

Everyone has different energetic desires that match their energetic needs—depending on their whole being as a body, mind, soul, consciousness, their timing of hunger, and their soul-journey. It is unique!

"I don't always - most likely never really - want to eat exactly at the same time when everyone else is eating—let alone sit around the table with everyone. Rather, I just fill my needs with exactly what I need, when I need it —then get back with speed to being occupied with something much more important, making myself happy through playing."

~ Your Child

It's a secret - or maybe not so secret - dream of every parent to have the whole family together around the table, being happy. Togetherness and conversation at a dinner table is a fun gathering of very high energetic value, but only if all involved truly want to BE there. All it takes is real family life scenarios to kick in; one who is not freely choosing to BE there, one who needs to go potty right now, one who is late getting home, one who is not feeling well, or one who is in a bad mood—and the energetic value is in the dumps.

Do you really still want to bet all your well-feeling coins on that dream of yours?

"Eating around the table as a family is more often than not me fulfilling your values that you have from growing up and your desire to be happy—but I am not here to fulfill that, I am here to experience my being and live my life to fulfill my needs."

~ *Your Child*

Parenting Through the Eyes of Lollipops means not making family dinner attendance a must. The funny fact with this is you get to watch how everyone suddenly - sooner or later - wants to BE there.

Peace takes over if beautiful family time together is not based on something that is loaded with old beliefs - like food, eating, and feeding time - or really any specifically planned time. There are so many different needs to be met in order for everyone to be happy, that if togetherness is grabbed when presented spontaneously, family time can be enjoyed more often.

What actions can you take?

Ask your children what kind of food they want to eat for breakfast, lunch, and dinner—and when. Plan ahead and let them choose what feels right for them. Great questions to ask are ones like:

"What would you like to eat, what would feel good to you?"

"What energy would you like to fill your body with right now?"

Then go make it for them, or even better, involve your children by letting them make it for themselves.

This might seem like a long stretch of intensive and difficult work, especially if you have a whole bunch of children to feed. But it only seems that way when seen through physical eyes because on an energetic soul-level, they get to nourish and fill themselves with the perfect energy and nutrients they need, keeping them balanced and happy—saving your energy in the long run, because we all know that unbalanced and grumpy children use up a whole lot more of you and your happiness than over the moon joyous children.

"I get to stay healthy because I fill up with exactly what I need. I get to know myself better by constantly having to choose what I want to eat. I grow

my creativity by coming up with what tastes yummy. I strengthen my confidence by practicing my capability to know who I really am and by speaking up for myself to choose differently than others. This makes for a strong mind, a strong soul connection, a deep knowing, and a rock solid intuition inside of me."

~ *Your Child*

Yes, this could mean that you have three different menus cooking at once if everyone wants to eat something different. It might even feel like you are losing your mind at times. That is when thinking about - and focusing on - all the created happiness, balance, and yumminess is better than looking in disbelief at your over-used stove. Smile, parents, smile!

"Think about the opening of all possibilities and freedom for you too—you get to be yourself, and eat whatever you want at whatever time is right for you."

~ *Your Child*

What are you waiting for, go make the food that your heart desires too—no more eating what everyone else is eating! Enjoy your new created freedom.

Teach your children early on how to make their own food and involve them in the cooking, so that they can take over the food preparation and play in the soul-ful garden of fulfilling their needs at an early age—happy children guaranteed!

"Don't worry, I will not only choose sweets and candy! When given an education of the foods available and the chance to choose and decide, I will want to make good choices. The ones that turn out to be not so good, I will take them like a champ and hold on tight to the knowing that they made me happy when I devoured them."

~ *Your Child*

Keep in mind that the change in the job taking and filling for who the spiritual and who the physical teachers or students are is a constant one, so be on alert Mom and Dad.

Your children are speedsters!

If trouble arises, stop and ask yourself honestly:

"Am I filling the right job right now?"

"Am I studying the right subject right now?"

"Is my child teaching me physically or spiritually right now?"

"Am I dancing a harmonious dance with my child?"

To harmonize, quit the unfitting job that you are holding on for dear life, and with your deepest gratitude, go fill the right and fitting one for right now. No harm done, just a bit of clarity needed and a wonderful adjustment accomplished!

This IS Parenting Through the Eyes of Lollipops!

GO TO BED, SHOWER, BRUSH YOUR TEETH

"When I fiercely resist the what, the how, or the when of things that you make me do, I resist with great reasons—because it is not perfectly fitting for me!"

~ Your Child

Visualize a world where everyone is forced to go to bed when told—meaning, you drop everything; give up your creative thoughts, quiet your wonderful laughter and joy, and definitely stop the powerful learning that you are in right now, to always very peacefully and agreeably go to bed. Now imagine everyone being happy in that world—you too, Mom and Dad!

This would not be possible!

"Instead of thinking that I am a rebellious or difficult child and getting angry at me, please understand that when I refuse it's because you are asking me to not live my truth. I am just standing up to BE me here!"

~ Your Child

Parenting Through the Eyes of Lollipops shifts this to something like this:

Feel how incredible everyone's own expansion is in an environment where there is complete trust in every soul being to choose the right bedtime - brush-teeth-time or shower-time - for themselves. Feel the happiness, peacefulness, and well-feeling energy that is created, shared, and spread to everyone and everything in a place of such free-choosing-magic.

Wouldn't you want to live there?

Imagine and feel yourself being in this happy world and notice your sudden energy burst, your immediate smile, your lightness and playfulness, and your wonderfully rock solid connection to your soul being—all by being so free.

More often than not you can meet your child in the middle of what you are expecting and your child is standing up for, but best is when you can change the what, when, and how to match your child's soul calling—their deepest needs. Who knows, you might find that their solution is a much more blessed and better way for you too—which has happened to me on countless occasions.

"I get it, sometimes I have to do the what, the when, and the how that you are asking of me because it has to be that way. I might not like it, but I get it. After all, I am a sophisticated soul being."

~ Your Child

There is no spoiling your children in these situations! Well, maybe spoiling them to BE them, because you allow your children to BE, to live their truth, and to grow their inner soul-wisdom—making you an enabler and supporter of a connected, peaceful, and loving human being that will be grateful for this free way of upbringing for the rest of their physical lives and beyond. A spoiling-greatness indeed, and know that this will spoil you to grow and remember your soul-freedom too, you spoiled soul, you!

"When we fight and things are not wonderfully good between us, it is a tempting and easy way, for you to look at me, thinking, what is wrong with that kid?"

~ Your Child

If the above thought process is yours, you are invited by the most powerful energetic forces to go and read, and re-read, and re-re-read the section in this book called It Is Never The Child! Because it really never is. Rather, your feelings and expectations are old habits - old beliefs - that are imprinted in your ways of parenting—while your child is simply following their soul calling and mirroring to you what is there for you to feel, look at, solve, unblock, love, accept, respect, appreciate, thank, heal, and take responsibility for.

"As soon as you take responsibility for your feelings, I can stop being your mirror in that iffy situation between us—I can stop being rebellious about it!"

~ *Your Child*

Ask yourself:

"Why is the refusal of my child so difficult for me?"

"What does my child's resistance have to do with me?"

"What feelings are there for me to feel?"

"What am I feeling?"

Acknowledge the answers that come up for you with bravery, and know that you can conquer this as the strong and powerful soul being - parent - that you are. I say, put on your suit of armor, hop on your warrior horse, and ride into the soul-ful "Ready to BE me!" sunset. I promise you, it will be worth it and you will be happy that you did.

If you decide to hold on to your old ways or look away from the gift this rebellious behavior of your child represents, the un-wellness with your children can get bigger, stronger, or pop up as new issues in disguise—resulting in you not dancing a harmonious dance with your children. In this case, you are not taking advantage of the learning and healing opportunity this holds for you since the rebellion is mirroring you something that is yours.

Keep in mind that the change in the job taking and filling for who the spiritual and who the physical teachers or students are is a constant one, so be on alert Mom and Dad.

Your children are speedsters!

If trouble arises, stop and ask yourself honestly:

"Am I filling the right job right now?"

"Am I studying the right subject right now?"

"Is my child teaching me physically or spiritually right now?"

"Am I dancing a harmonious dance with my child?"

To harmonize, quit the unfitting job that you are holding on for dear life, and with your deepest gratitude, go fill the right and fitting one for right now. No harm done, just a bit of clarity needed and a wonderful adjustment accomplished!

This IS Parenting Through the Eyes of Lollipops!

PUNISHMENTS — CONSEQUENCES

"Well, I'm here to tell you that punishments simply don't work. Even if I end up following your rules, I only do it because of the punishment—not because I agree."

~ Your Child

Punishments are an awkward dance - contrary to a harmonious dance - that is moving parents through the fuel of anger, resentment, feeling disrespected, and a whole lot of disagreement that is present. They shift children to shut themselves off and to not care anymore. How else can they cope with feelings of being misunderstood, treated unfairly, and being lower than the parents on the scale of importance?

Think about it… Children have a natural deep soul-knowing that their souls are as equal as their parents, making a punishment - which is degrading - something that's not even the slightest bit okay on their radar, whereas the parents think that they are teaching their children, yet forgetting - or not even having the slightest clue - that their children are equals, souls just like them.

Nobody is happy in this, nobody can be happy that way!

Finding out what your child needs, what your child feels, and what your child wants is always more effective than any punishment you can come up with, because in the heat of the moment you and your child are not coming from the same understanding and knowing—which is that you are both co-creating as equals with each other.

"It soothes my inner tiger when you treat me as an equal—I calm down and can feel my love for you. Don't you want that for you and me?"

~ Your Child

Consequences, on the other hand, have a more natural vibe: "If you do this, then this might be the cleanup situation you are looking at…" However, since everyone creates their physical reality, even consequences are not set in stone and can be shifted to be gifts and opportunities. For example, have you ever chosen something, then thought it was not the right choice after all, only for it to turn out to be the best thing that ever happened for you?

So where punishments are degrading and given by the parents from an unhelpful emotional frequency, consequences are given by the situation or by life itself—letting your children learn smoothly and more naturally.

For instance, "You are grounded because you returned home late" is a punishment that is given by the parents, with not much learning happening here, whereas; "Coming home late means you are not getting enough sleep—the end result being, you are exhausted" is a consequence that is given by the situation—providing plenty of learning for your child.

Keep in mind that the change in the job taking and filling for who the spiritual and who the physical teachers or students are is a constant one, so be on alert Mom and Dad.

Your children are speedsters!

If trouble arises, stop and ask yourself honestly:

"Am I filling the right job right now?"

"Am I studying the right subject right now?"

"Is my child teaching me physically or spiritually right now?"

"Am I dancing a harmonious dance with my child?"

To harmonize, quit the unfitting job that you are holding on for dear life, and with your deepest gratitude, go fill the right and fitting one for right now. No harm done, just a bit of clarity needed and a wonderful adjustment accomplished!

This IS Parenting Through the Eyes of Lollipops!

BUT WHAT ABOUT RULES?

"As long as what I am doing is not of a life-threatening nature... What rules? Who made up the existing rules anyways? Out of which antique beliefs did they emerge, and what an incredible expansion could it be if you and I would make new rules together?"

~ Your Child

Rules are only harmonious if they make sense to everyone, are talked over, and are explained in detail—best is if they are agreed upon by all involved. If the rules aid the family living needs and are making the community of family-life work better or smoother, they are easy to follow because they don't seem like rules. On the other hand, enforcing rules because you the parent said so never works and never creates harmony in your soul-to-soul relationship with your children.

Your family is a community living situation—a soul-ful co-creation of living together!

Family meetings in which you discuss the community living arrangement and the meaning of the rules that you would like to create are great for rule-making. For example, "In order for our family to work smooth, this is what needs to happen. How can we do that?" Everyone IS equal in this situation—a guaranteed incredible outcome!

"For silly-ness... In the world of vacuums it looks something like this: would you rather want a vacuum that you have to guide, push, and with lots of effort make go places, or a vacuum that is automatic—you set it down and it just goes, all alone, doing its thing?"

~ Your Child

Being the rule-maker and then having to always guide, push, and make your children do things, go places, or say something, is very exhausting over time. It also shows a lack of trust from the parents' side—hint, hint, the gold nugget here is for you to grow your trust in yourself, the world, and in your children.

"Sure, sometimes you have to mingle in my business of becoming; turn me around, help me move forward, push me over an obstacle or out of the way of one coming at me… But do we really have to be so rule based—asking for so many disagreements? Or can we just modernize our rules together?"

~ *Your Child*

In the situation of a child not doing the best to keep the community living healthy and flowing - following the agreed rules - find out the reason.

Has the child changed and expanded to BE and live a more fitting self—yet, you are not caught up with them?

Is the way that things are set old, outdated, and/or are the rules expired?

Were the child's boundaries crossed by something that was said or happened?

Does the child feel like less, while knowing that they are equal?

Taking a situation at face value without questioning the child means your child will jump back on board to follow the agreed rules in no time—given that the fitting changes are made ASAP.

"Rules are out of style! Respect, love, and equality is in style!"

~ *Your Child*

Maybe you can sit over a licking-lollipop-session as a family and talk about all these silly rules, while giggling your souls out, then with playful seriousness put new rules into place that fit all souls involved—if, after all that laughter, you even still need the rules!

"Mom, Dad, do you really think that without rules I would be a wild, unpleasant, and out-of control child—an unlikable soul being?

~ *Your Child*

Keep in mind that the change in the job taking and filling for who the spiritual and who the physical teachers or students are is a constant one, so be on alert Mom and Dad.

Your children are speedsters!

If trouble arises, stop and ask yourself honestly:

"Am I filling the right job right now?"

"Am I studying the right subject right now?"

"Is my child teaching me physically or spiritually right now?"

"Am I dancing a harmonious dance with my child?"

To harmonize, quit the unfitting job that you are holding on for dear life, and with your deepest gratitude, go fill the right and fitting one for right now. No harm done, just a bit of clarity needed and a wonderful adjustment accomplished!

This IS Parenting Through the Eyes of Lollipops!

WHEN ONE HAS A HARD TIME

"No matter the why, what, when, or who, it's very clear that when one is not nice, not happy, not balanced, not helpful, or loving, that one is having a hard time."

~ Your Child

Supporting a child who is in distress by surrounding them with love and understanding and making sure they hear, feel, and see this "pulling together" as a whole family, does the trick to uplift them every time—and very speedily, indeed.

Why? Because carrying hardship alone is much harder and heavier than being together with warriors who fill the individual with love, kindness, positive viewpoints, and uplifting reminders of the soul that they are.

This choice of support also goes a long way in defusing the already heated situation - no matter the why - and lifts the soul in distress to its rightful place of well-feeling—matching all the other souls who already are well-feeling. Think of the grand party this is, with all these happy family members - souls - in one place.

A lot of times the distress and the non-aligned behavior dissolves in the sand with this approach - without even being consciously solved - because that support is a powerful love that rises and drenches everyone and everything in well-being energy —stronger than any problem in the whole wide world.

"Tell me that when I am in distress everyone will pull together as a family to support and uplift me. Promise me that we will solve this together and that I am not alone!"

~ Your Child

Keep in mind that the change in the job taking and filling for who the spiritual and who the physical teachers or students are is a constant one, so be on alert Mom and Dad.

Your children are speedsters!

If trouble arises, stop and ask yourself honestly:

"Am I filling the right job right now?"

"Am I studying the right subject right now?"

"Is my child teaching me physically or spiritually right now?"

"Am I dancing a harmonious dance with my child?"

To harmonize, quit the unfitting job that you are holding on for dear life, and with your deepest gratitude, go fill the right and fitting one for right now. No harm done, just a bit of clarity needed and a wonderful adjustment accomplished!

This IS Parenting Through the Eyes of Lollipops!

IS YOUR CHILD LISTENING?

"When I don't listen, it's because you are not listening!"

~ Your Child

Here is a picture that is very familiar: the parent talks to the child, the child is not listening, the parent gets frustrated and maybe even angry, the child is still not listening… and on it goes like a merry-go-round.

Saying to a child "You are not listening!" is like saying to your car "You are not driving!" when all along you forgot to fill the gas tank, did not put the key in, aren't starting the car, and haven't been pushing the gas pedal—the car will always have a reason for why it is not starting.

So do your children! They always have their own reasons why they are not listening. Here are a few examples of why:

Is what you are saying really just not that interesting? Re-think what you are saying.

Is the child busy in its own happiness? Leave the happy being to be happy.

Is the child not able to hear—are they tired, hungry, or sick? Help your child fill their needs.

Is the child's soul-reasoning not heard by you? Listen and feel into what their reasons are.

Mold yourself to become the master of recognizing the signs that your child - their soul - is giving you. Some of these signs are as tiny as a grain of salt and catching them is asking for all of your undivided attention. When caught at such a tiny size and then immediately fixed, they shift swiftly. Others are more like a huge meteorite coming straight at you. When they are already this size, you definitely need to get all your soul-wisdom together to figure things out fast—to avoid that meteorite hitting you. But you can do it, because you are that powerful of a reason-detective.

Keep in mind that the change in the job taking and filling for who the spiritual and who the physical teachers or students are is a constant one, so be on alert Mom and Dad.

Your children are speedsters!

If trouble arises, stop and ask yourself honestly:

"Am I filling the right job right now?"

"Am I studying the right subject right now?"

"Is my child teaching me physically or spiritually right now?"

"Am I dancing a harmonious dance with my child?"

To harmonize, quit the unfitting job that you are holding on for dear life, and with your deepest gratitude, go fill the right and fitting one for right now. No harm done, just a bit of clarity needed and a wonderful adjustment accomplished!

This IS Parenting Through the Eyes of Lollipops!

ANGER

"So here's the deal with anger… For some it might be a sign of weakness, of not being in emotional control, needing help, or simply just being bad or hard headed. But for me it is a very powerful part of me, a kind of warrior energy, showing how strong and powerful I can be."

~ *Your Child*

As the parent you are the physical life teacher for your angry child, teaching them that they can't just run around like warriors and anger-splash anything and anyone that is in their way.

"Sometimes I get angry when I feel boxed in. Please be patient with me! Other times I am angry when something goes against my soul calling. I am really studying hard on this anger thing, promise."

~ *Your Child*

To keep the balance, your children shift to be the spiritual teachers because you need to find new and creative ways to explain to your children that feeling anger is okay, that living it, owning it, and accepting it is healthy, and that it never needs to be buried or stay unused, but never released on others—a wonderful healing opportunity for your own anger-experiences from your younger years.

"I burn up fast, meaning I become one with my anger mode at light-speed. That's because I am very new to this physical world—I have a lot to fight for since I am new and want to carve my way, my life, and my personality to fit my truth."

~ *Your Child*

When anger gets the better part of your child, there are two ways to handle it:

Fuel their anger by using your own personal anger to add on top of your child's anger—building the Eiffel Tower of anger.

Or better…

Soothe your child's warrior energy of anger by seeing your child through the eyes of your soul being—through pure positive energy. Anger is an only-in-physical-life emotion.

The soothing really depends on the age of your child. A hug or ice cream soothes any early age warrior, but wanting to hug your angry teenager will make this already huge tower even bigger, which is a no-go. Adding to their bank account is more of the right soothing type—works like magic for them. Remember, money is energy—just like a hug is. Giving your teenager the energy of money means you are filling their energetic needs while matching their desires at this point in their life.

"If I ask for money, it matches the energy that I am in need of in order to be happy—a match for my soul calling."

~ Your Teenager

To get the right feeling here:

Imagine yourself being angry. Stay there for a bit to amplify your angry-ness. Now visualize someone walking up to you and giving you bubble gum with the expectation that it will soothe your inner warrior. You look at them in disbelief, getting angrier as they speak.

In another scenario, someone walks up to you giving you the keys to your dream car—the one that's perfect for you in this time of your life. You will soothe-up immediately and shift to BE and live the mood of happiness, gratitude, appreciation, joy, excitement, and "it's not all that bad."

There's no difference for your teenagers, they love money— it's like oil for a machine for them. Money is the energetic match to their desires and their soul-being!

To further explain…

Money is energy, it vibrates in the frequency of abundance,

and when loved it carries the added energy of love—matching the frequency of pure positive energy that every soul being is. When money is hated or negatively looked at, the abundance is overridden by the energy of negativity—not matching a soul's essence, and explaining why money can be negative or bad for some.

When you make your children happy by gifting them money coming from your heart, you gift them something that is a perfect energetic match to their soul being—in a sense, you help them live in their soul essence.

But enough of the energy called money, and back to the beauty of anger!

Acknowledge anger as a powerful warrior energy that is present in every physical being and in all of physical life. At times it can be the best alarm signal—like getting angry because your soul does not agree with boundaries being overstepped by others, and through this powerful strength, you react. The perfect usage of this energy! Shutting anger down - or out - means that you shut a great part of yourself down and turn off your protective alarm signal. Plus, have you ever cleaned your house while being angry? If so then you know how much speed this anger can give you—you can get it done in no time!

"When I am grumpy, know that my grumpy-ness is mine and has nothing to do with you—even if I happen to be mad at you. Meaning, separating yourself from my moody-ness ensures that you can stay neutral and support me from there."

~ Your Child

Accepting, respecting, appreciating, thanking, and loving the anger in yourself and in your children means that you love yourself as a whole being, and love your children as whole beings. I say love your anger as a grand part of you—and know that it's all about the conscious understanding and perfect usage of it!

Keep in mind that the change in the job taking and filling for who the spiritual and who the physical teachers or students are is a constant one, so be on alert Mom and Dad.

Your children are speedsters!

If trouble arises, stop and ask yourself honestly:

"Am I filling the right job right now?"

"Am I studying the right subject right now?"

"Is my child teaching me physically or spiritually right now?"

"Am I dancing a harmonious dance with my child?"

To harmonize, quit the unfitting job that you are holding on for dear life, and with your deepest gratitude, go fill the right and fitting one for right now. No harm done, just a bit of clarity needed and a wonderful adjustment accomplished!

This IS Parenting Through the Eyes of Lollipops!

THE BEAUTY OF ONLY CARING ABOUT THEMSELVES

"Yes, I really do only care about myself, because that is my only responsibility and my reason to BE and live in this physical life. With this determination, I offer you a view into your own magic of being self-centered and self-caring."

~ Your Child

Imagine a world where it is law to always and only care about someone else! You don't exist for yourself, your needs are not important, and your desires—what the heck are desires? Even though someone in that lump of selfless caretakers will eventually care about you, it's never going to be truly in the right way, because it's not you taking care of you.

Parenting Through the Eyes of Lollipops shifts this to become more like this:

Imagine a world where everyone takes full and complete responsibility of themselves by taking exceptional care of their happiness, needs, and desires, putting their focus on being the best person they can BE—constantly fueling up with self love, self respect, self confidence, and self care while recycling that pure energy to keep taking great care of themselves. Everyone is pure in their truth - not filled with anyone else's things - and deeply connected with their inner being by living from their gracious space; a true place where everyone is at their highest potential and able to co-create magic.

What a world to BE and live in!

"I am so deeply connected to my self-care that it bothers me infinitely when I am not feeling good—making my self-centeredness unstoppable. That is just what I promised myself when entering my physical life. So don't try to limit it!"

~ *Your Child*

Your child teaches you spiritually with their self-centeredness to take full responsibility of yourself, and to make yourself and your wellbeing your number one priority. BE selfish!

"When I am showing you and others loud and clear - maybe even with fists - that I am not happy, I am truly just taking care of myself, my needs, and my wellbeing by rebelling against the non-fitting."

~ *Your Child*

Physically, you teach your child that it is a wonderful cause to care about others as well—by demonstrating to them the kindness, helpfulness, and graciousness that comes from a well-taken-care-of heart.

Keep in mind that the change in the job taking and filling for who the spiritual and who the physical teachers or students are is a constant one, so be on alert Mom and Dad.

Your children are speedsters!

If trouble arises, stop and ask yourself honestly:

"Am I filling the right job right now?"

"Am I studying the right subject right now?"

"Is my child teaching me physically or spiritually right now?"

"Am I dancing a harmonious dance with my child?"

To harmonize, quit the unfitting job that you are holding on for dear life, and with your deepest gratitude, go fill the right and fitting one for right now. No harm done, just a bit of clarity needed and a wonderful adjustment accomplished!

This IS Parenting Through the Eyes of Lollipops!

I WANT MORE—ALWAYS

"I want more and more because that IS what the expansion of physical life is all about, besides experiencing the excitement I promised myself while being here!"

~ *Your Child*

Imagine wanting something and once you have it, you never have any further wantings again—ever! You are done! That would be silly, no?

What's not silly is to imagine that there are no limits to your wantings. That whatever you want you can have, and that with every new wanting you expand to climb the ladder of physical life higher and higher, happier and happier, smarter and smarter, richer and richer, and wiser and wiser.

That IS as you expected it to be when you decided to come here!

"I am here to crush it—by living my life through wanting more in order to expand more! I am not spoiled, greedy, or wanting too much—that is your old way of thinking. In my new and fresh book of physical life, your old beliefs and rules that create such discord have no voice."

~ *Your Child*

Your children are here to live extraordinary lives and so are you!

Them wanting more is based on their deep soul-knowing that they are deserving and that there is always more—for everyone. They understand that the natural flow of physical life IS always "What's next? What's more? What's new? What's better?"

Wanting more from a space of gratitude and appreciation for what IS creates more mindful happiness—a well-feeling that is the matching expansion to your soul essence and the reason that you are here in this physical life. So doesn't it make sense for you to follow your children and give this "wanting more" a try sometime too?

Your children's constant new wantings are your spiritual "behind kicker" to remember that you, too, deserve more and also really want more. You, on the other hand, are their physical professor—teaching them math and budgeting in physical life. Remember though, money is energy, and all energy is limitless and expandable. Keep this teaching light for yourself and for your children.

"You don't always have to say yes to all my wantings, and maybe you can't. I get that! However, if you use me wanting more to climb your own ladder of happiness, meaning you want more for yourself too, we will create more—it's law!"

~ *Your Child*

Keep in mind that the change in the job taking and filling for who the spiritual and who the physical teachers or students are is a constant one, so be on alert Mom and Dad.

Your children are speedsters!

If trouble arises, stop and ask yourself honestly:

"Am I filling the right job right now?"

"Am I studying the right subject right now?"

"Is my child teaching me physically or spiritually right now?"

"Am I dancing a harmonious dance with my child?"

To harmonize, quit the unfitting job that you are holding on for dear life, and with your deepest gratitude, go fill the right and fitting one for right now. No harm done, just a bit of clarity needed and a wonderful adjustment accomplished!

This IS Parenting Through the Eyes of Lollipops!

BOUNDARIES

"Imagine a life where you are pushed, and pushed, and pushed to get incredible practice to learn how to set your own boundaries—clearly, strongly, and soul-fully!"

~ Your Child

Your children will, at certain times, push you to your absolute maximum! But remember, your children can never make you do anything. They mirror you something that is in you—that you are ready to see, hear, feel, think, heal, cleanse, and take responsibility of.

About that "max" of yours:

You are limitless! Your maximum that you are perceiving right now is not even a real limit. You have the capability of expanding and because of that, you will just amplify yourself to newfound limits. Which, again, are not real…

"Do I enjoy watching you at your limit? No! However, I don't feel for you, because if I would I could not be the messenger and pusher that I promised to BE when coming into your life."

~ Your Child

Your children's pushing invites you on a spiritual level to gain more self-worth by tickling your realization of your always present worthiness, initiating your expansion to set new fitting boundaries for you—something that you might never really got a chance to practice and get good at while growing up.

Embrace those "I am at my max" moments because they help you to make a huge nest-egg of your own fitting boundaries, and teach you that you can always go further than you thought you could.

"Don't get comfy; just when you think you are set and balanced, I will find another push to give. That is what I promised when arriving in your

life!"

~ *Your Child*

You, on the other hand, are showing your children how to set those boundaries in physical life—by watching you set your boundaries, they see first-hand how respect IS created, because respect can never be demanded, but only created by living your own self-respect.

"Mom, Dad, set your new boundaries fast so I can stop pushing—at least until I am called into my next pushing job."

~ *Your Child*

Keep in mind that the change in the job taking and filling for who the spiritual and who the physical teachers or students are is a constant one, so be on alert Mom and Dad.

Your children are speedsters!

If trouble arises, stop and ask yourself honestly:

"Am I filling the right job right now?"

"Am I studying the right subject right now?"

"Is my child teaching me physically or spiritually right now?"

"Am I dancing a harmonious dance with my child?"

To harmonize, quit the unfitting job that you are holding on for dear life, and with your deepest gratitude, go fill the right and fitting one for right now. No harm done, just a bit of clarity needed and a wonderful adjustment accomplished!

This IS Parenting Through the Eyes of Lollipops!

QUESTIONS

"Questions are great when I am the one asking you, but not so great when you are the one asking me."

~ *Your Tweener and Teenager*

When they are little they ask you millions of questions, and millions of times it is the same one—if you celebrate every one of them like a token of gold, you get to celebrate millions of times.

These questions are like a love-glue that is strengthening your relationship with your little one, because you get to fill these smart minds - and wise souls - with physical life knowledge, words of love, and well-feeling energy—creating closeness and solid trust. Gold!

But just as the value of gold changes over time, the value of questions and questioning change with the age of your children. At first, you get an unlimited allowance of asking questions, so ask away because that will not always be the case. Once your child is in their teens - maybe even before that - your freedom to ask will be restricted by them, and once overstepped they will let you know that very clearly. Since your question is pointed at them - meaning you want to know something about them and their life - it's you who then needs to stay fair and square by putting a stop to your pesky questions.

It's recommended that you accept your child's reaction with the knowing that your gold has not lost its value forever, the worth has just plummeted for now until the demand rises again —which it will! Then ask away.

If you ask questions to make conversation with your teenager because otherwise there is only stillness in the room, stillness is still the better choice. That stillness holds immense magic and power for you because you can visualize them at their highest potential—and in silence share that pure positive energy you see in them by filling every single cell of their whole being to the brim and into overflow. This works because everyone and everything is energy and constantly sharing energies with each other.

Sometimes no words are needed—yet, powerful shifts are still accomplished.

If by any chance the unthinkable opportunity of making fun conversation with your teenager - without asking those pesky questions - is presented to you, go for it and milk it for all that it's worth.

And just to throw this in there, there is also the magical invention called text messages in which you can ask, remind, inform, or teach your teenagers valuable things without pestering them—they can read your words in solitude, they can let them sink in, and they can keep their dignity by reacting in private.

Keep in mind that the change in the job taking and filling for who the spiritual and who the physical teachers or students are is a constant one, so be on alert Mom and Dad.

Your children are speedsters!

If trouble arises, stop and ask yourself honestly:

"Am I filling the right job right now?"

"Am I studying the right subject right now?"

"Is my child teaching me physically or spiritually right now?"

"Am I dancing a harmonious dance with my child?"

To harmonize, quit the unfitting job that you are holding on for dear life, and with your deepest gratitude, go fill the right and fitting one for right now. No harm done, just a bit of clarity needed and a wonderful adjustment accomplished!

This IS Parenting Through the Eyes of Lollipops!

WHEN PARENTS SAY "NO!"

"When you say no, you are closing a gate that could lead to new and different experiences!"

~ *Your Child*

Saying the word "No!" for dangerous, hurtful, painful, unlawful, abusive, and overstepped boundaries is a "must" teaching that you want to pass on to your children and encourage them to use. "No!" carries the energy of: Stop, enough, putting up barriers, finish, and stepping up for yourself.

Try it and say, "No!" with determination, power, and strength —maybe even try stomping your feet to amplify this.

Acknowledge how strong this feels for you and the energetic shift that is taking place in you. That IS how powerful of an energy the word "No!" is or can be, and also what the word "No!" was and is intended for.

Saying "No!" to your child wanting ice cream is a bit overrated when understanding that, because you are literally putting up a barrier to the ice cream and shifting yourself and your children to feel the strong frequency of the word "No!"

For a situation like that softening your "No!" by creatively coming up with other words, finding other ways, or maybe even making a compromise would be more fitting. Why not both of you break the rules and have that ice cream together?

Use "No!" wisely, and choose a gentler way to communicate as much as you can. That's all there really is to understand with this powerful little word.

Keep in mind that the change in the job taking and filling for who the spiritual and who the physical teachers or students are is a constant one, so be on alert Mom and Dad.

Your children are speedsters!

If trouble arises, stop and ask yourself honestly:

"Am I filling the right job right now?"

"Am I studying the right subject right now?"

"Is my child teaching me physically or spiritually right now?"

"Am I dancing a harmonious dance with my child?"

To harmonize, quit the unfitting job that you are holding on for dear life, and with your deepest gratitude, go fill the right and fitting one for right now. No harm done, just a bit of clarity needed and a wonderful adjustment accomplished!

This IS Parenting Through the Eyes of Lollipops!

COMPLIMENTS

"Compliment me endlessly—don't hold back, ever!"

~ Your Child

Compliments are a soul-ful way of spreading love and light to yourself - you are the one starting this goodness after all - to the one you are complimenting, and to the whole world by sharing and spreading this well-feeling energy.

Compliments shift everyone and everything to BE and live in a high-for-life frequency!

That's why you are invited to compliment yourself! Yes, you read this right, have over-the-top compliment chit-chats with yourself. Best is while smiling and looking at yourself in the mirror.

Then go and compliment your children, all the time— drenching them in your well-meaning words to lift them higher and higher into happiness. Watch them soar!

Compliment the lady at the grocery store, the birds, your car... Say these golden words out loud so your children can hear you—showing them how they too can lift everyone and everything up by showering the world with compliments.

Keep in mind that the change in the job taking and filling for who the spiritual and who the physical teachers or students are is a constant one, so be on alert Mom and Dad.

Your children are speedsters!

If trouble arises, stop and ask yourself honestly:

"Am I filling the right job right now?"

"Am I studying the right subject right now?"

"Is my child teaching me physically or spiritually right now?"

"Am I dancing a harmonious dance with my child?"

To harmonize, quit the unfitting job that you are holding on for dear life, and with your deepest gratitude, go fill the right and fitting one for right now. No harm done, just a bit of clarity needed and a wonderful adjustment accomplished!

This IS Parenting Through the Eyes of Lollipops!

STANDING YOUR PARENTAL GROUND

"Choose to stand up for yourself with the purpose of whether it feels true for you or not, Mom and Dad, instead of because you are my parent, or because you said so."

~ Your Child

Standing your ground means:

BE true to your soul being by following your soul-calling—by what feels good for you and by standing tall and proud for who you really are.

Standing your parental ground does not mean:

Stand harshly and stubbornly by what you said just because you are the parent, because you said so, because you are/want to be right, or because "those are the rules." When you stand up for yourself, your beliefs, and your opinions in that way, you are being and living way off of your true soul existence—acting out the opposite of standing up for yourself. That is why this never feels good for you or anyone and it's why your children rebel. They can see right through you—soul-to-soul!

Before you stand up for yourself, become really clear of who you really are, of what feels good for you, and what it is that you really want. Ask yourself, "Are my reasons pure?" and from there make your case while consciously listening to your children and your soul wisdom.

Notice how they react to you standing up—they are a truth barometer of how soul-fitting your standing up really is for you. Do they accept it? Then it's pure. Do they rebel against it? Then it's not pure, or your rules are outdated. Accomplish the necessary shifts and try again.

Together, or shall we say soul-to-soul, take this opportunity of a deliciously truthful expansion and make it fitting for both of you.

Keep in mind that the change in the job taking and filling for who the spiritual and who the physical teachers or students are is a constant one, so be on alert Mom and Dad.

Your children are speedsters!

If trouble arises, stop and ask yourself honestly:

"Am I filling the right job right now?"

"Am I studying the right subject right now?"

"Is my child teaching me physically or spiritually right now?"

"Am I dancing a harmonious dance with my child?"

To harmonize, quit the unfitting job that you are holding on for dear life, and with your deepest gratitude, go fill the right and fitting one for right now. No harm done, just a bit of clarity needed and a wonderful adjustment accomplished!

This IS Parenting Through the Eyes of Lollipops!

DECISIONS

"I want to decide for myself because I CAN decide for myself! I got this!"

~ Your Child

As babies they decide that their full diaper does not feel good; you accept that decision by graciously changing them to be clean again. They also decide that they are hungry; you respect that decision and happily feed them—and they decide that they need attention; you hear their decision, and with a smile, dance the monkey dance for them to soothe their needs.

Then your children grow up and want to keep deciding, but now they want to decide more and bigger things for themselves —decisions beyond full diapers, being hungry, or needing attention. That is when the greatest decision making opportunities are presented to them—an incredible time of learning that helps them to grow into professionally-trained decision makers.

Yet, that is usually when parents pull the plug by meeting them with millions of rules, plenty of no's, and loads of decisions that are made for them. What in the lollipop just happened?

"Am I not cute enough anymore? Am I not smart enough anymore? Mom, Dad, please explain, why are we going backwards here?"

~ Your Child

Your children rebel because they want to keep their birthright of making their own decisions, and rightfully so! You might say, "But they are only children and don't know yet!"

"I am a soul, outfitted with deep inner-knowing, always with great guidance, and limitless wisdom! I only learn to use it better if I am allowed to make my own decisions!"

~ Your Child

Letting your children make their own decisions as much as possible means that you let them expand into their truth as much as possible—while showing that you trust in their capability to live their lives on their own terms, which is an empowering way for your children to grow up.

I say let's not only let them make their decisions, but also strengthen their decision making!

Ask them every day, "What do you want to eat?" and "What do you want to do?" or "What would feel better for you?" and "What do you want to wear?" or "What do you love?"

The beautiful benefit here is that this constantly shifts them to BE and live in their deepest truth - their soul essence - while learning incredible things about themselves, being encouraged to feel themselves, and as a result can find out who they really are— one of the most rock-solid gifts you can give to your children!

"I know what I want to eat!

I know when I want to go to bed!

I know when and who I want to hug and smile at!

I know that I love you!"

~ Your Child

Letting them choose takes a load off your shoulders and lets you relax—because parenthood is now a co-creation versus a solo-parent-creation. Plus, you get to joyously witness them grow into being and living their strong-mindedness, a phenomenal personality trait that supports living a life that is exceptional—a great reassurance for you.

They teach you as spiritual teachers how you too can take the liberty to claim your birthright to decide well for yourself, shifting you to be their physical teacher by demonstrating them what good decisions are - or could be - in this physical life.

Once your children have made their decisions, they can easily switch to be your physical teachers by inspiring you through their grand decisions to go for your biggest life dreams too. For balance's sake, this offers you an opportunity to be the spiritual teacher by showering them with your gratitude and appreciation for being your inspiration. I say decide big for yourself, then drench your children in that deep admiration.

Keep in mind that the change in the job taking and filling for who the spiritual and who the physical teachers or students are is a constant one, so be on alert Mom and Dad.

Your children are speedsters!

If trouble arises, stop and ask yourself honestly:

"Am I filling the right job right now?"

"Am I studying the right subject right now?"

"Is my child teaching me physically or spiritually right now?"

"Am I dancing a harmonious dance with my child?"

To harmonize, quit the unfitting job that you are holding on for dear life, and with your deepest gratitude, go fill the right and fitting one for right now. No harm done, just a bit of clarity needed and a wonderful adjustment accomplished!

This IS Parenting Through the Eyes of Lollipops!

FIGHTING — NOT PHYSICALLY THOUGH

"I certainly unleash the warrior energy of fighting in you, don't I? That is part of the promise I made when coming into your life!"

~ *Your Child*

Fighting is not always bad, just think of the possible expansion for change that fighting can bring, not to mention the energy that is released by fights—clearing the air, if you will. It can be a beautiful cleansing - when fought properly and fairly - for everyone involved if fights are acknowledged, accepted, respected, appreciated, thanked, and loved for the opportunities that they really are.

Of course, if possible, give your best to solve any happening in peace—however, give yourself the chance to consciously choose "if or if not" you want to join the fight that your child has in store for you.

To think this through, ask yourself the following:

- Do I want to join this fight my child is offering to me because this fight is worth fighting for me—for the reason that it is good for me? Then we will fight back and forth together to strengthen mine and my child's warrior energy to the point where we both can feel and live the warrior power that we are.

- Do I want to stay in a high-for-life frequency and not join the fight by thinking or saying, "I love myself and I love you too much to fight this fight" instead? Here, I practice my strength to stay in my heart and the love for myself and my child. The harder my child fights, the more love I feel for the both of us. In case my jolly-ness makes my child even angrier, I know that it's a great practice for their warrior energy. Plus, they get to witness how I handle myself peacefully—great teaching high here!

"Fights should never happen, fights are always bad, solutions must

always be peaceful, or else... These old recordings are not true!"

~ Your Child

Make it of utmost importance that after the fight is over, you move on quickly and don't sulk in negative feelings towards yourself or the child. What was, was—it's not even true anymore, it's the past. You are fully in charge of creating a positive, happy, and well-feeling NOW, starting right now. Lollipops help a lot here!

Keep in mind that the change in the job taking and filling for who the spiritual and who the physical teachers or students are is a constant one, so be on alert Mom and Dad.

Your children are speedsters!

If trouble arises, stop and ask yourself honestly:

"Am I filling the right job right now?"

"Am I studying the right subject right now?"

"Is my child teaching me physically or spiritually right now?"

"Am I dancing a harmonious dance with my child?"

To harmonize, quit the unfitting job that you are holding on for dear life, and with your deepest gratitude, go fill the right and fitting one for right now. No harm done, just a bit of clarity needed and a wonderful adjustment accomplished!

Parents have full responsibility to stay proper—refrain from being mean, hurtful, abusive, diminishing, and soul-harming. Physically fighting with your children is never okay. Get help—for yourself and for your children!

This IS Parenting Through the Eyes of Lollipops!

FREEDOM

"Being free means that I am the happiest, being the happiest means that I am truly me, and being me means that I am doing what I came here to do!"

~ *Your Child*

Usually "freedom for kids" is thought of as them running around like wild animals without having any good behavior—which grows grey hairs on many adult heads because those thoughts are based on old beliefs, and when thought, they trigger the vision of old and untrue ways.

Just picture it:

Children running around like a wild bunch, acting like they don't care, and not in the slightest having any idea of their responsibility to behave. That immediately makes you think that this wacky version of them clearly needs rules to make them behave, so you make up rules. However, those guidelines are based on your old beliefs. Guess how that will go?

Your children will rebel and all freedom is forgotten—nothing works.

To base parenting on old, untrue beliefs, backfires in real parenthood-life because they put an unreasonable, unreal, not-free, and distrusting energy into the air that is creating unwell feelings for all involved—keeping your children short-leashed and far off from living their best and happiest lives. This makes what you fear a reality—but not because your children are a wild bunch of beings, but because they are fighting to break the rules so they can breathe freely in their truth.

Here is what freedom looks like:

- Freedom for your kids is their freedom to BE and live who they really are

- Freedom for your kids is their choice to follow their soul calling

- Freedom for your kids is for you to dance the harmonious dance with them

- Freedom for your kids is for you to understand that it's never the child

- Freedom for your kids is for you to live the love cycle of parenthood

- Freedom for your kids is to let your children off the hook

- Freedom for your kids is to take full responsibility for your own feelings and being

I say, let them BE free and go claim your own freedom too—and together, BE that free bunch that you are all longing to BE.

Keep in mind that the change in the job taking and filling for who the spiritual and who the physical teachers or students are is a constant one, so be on alert Mom and Dad.

Your children are speedsters!

If trouble arises, stop and ask yourself honestly:

"Am I filling the right job right now?"

"Am I studying the right subject right now?"

"Is my child teaching me physically or spiritually right now?"

"Am I dancing a harmonious dance with my child?"

To harmonize, quit the unfitting job that you are holding on for dear life, and with your deepest gratitude, go fill the right and fitting one for right now. No harm done, just a bit of clarity needed and a wonderful adjustment accomplished!

This IS Parenting Through the Eyes of Lollipops!

TRUST

"There are really two types of trust notable for our relationship, one is the trust that we both have an inner guidance to live our lives to our highest potential, and the other is the trust in each other, that we are guiding each other at all times."

~ Your Child

Trust that we both have an inner guidance:

Your child is first and foremost a soul with an inner guidance, just like you—physical age and physical time being here is the only difference, which on a soul level never matters.

"You tell me that I am a child, so little and new to this world—I say, only true on the physical life level. Energetically, I am a soul—and for giggles, who knows? Maybe I was your parent once."

~ Your Child

Trusting in your children that they know best for themselves - with exceptions of danger, like a young child crossing the street - is of utmost importance for you and for them.

If they can feel your solid trust, they are free to make the best decisions for themselves without needing to rebel—while feeling your distrust has them under surveillance with them possibly choosing "wrong" just out of spite.

Their choices are also a great barometer for you to gauge how truthful your trust in them really is. If they are making good decisions, your trust is likely on point; in case of bad decisions, check your trust in them and adjust yourself—while expecting amazing results.

Trust in each other that we are guiding each other:

"Imagine me with a blindfold and that you are guiding me along a path. That is the safety I am looking for, and your purpose that you are looking

for!"

~ *Your Child*

Your children arrive in this life with the capacity to fully and completely trust in you; to trust that you guide them, teach them, and are giving your best for them—always with their highest well-being in mind.

Now turn this around...

"Imagine yourself with a blindfold and that I am guiding you along a path. That is the purpose that I promised to fulfill and the love that you are wishing for."

~ *Your Child*

Can you do it?

Most parents can't imagine this type of complete trust in their children because they don't realize that children are intelligent soul beings—and not just helplessly new here.

Trusting that you and your children are here to guide each other equally means that you are trusting in the harmonious dance—which you are here to co-creatively dance together.

"Mom, Dad, please understand that your trust starts in you and for you, and then spills over into trusting that I am trustworthy in ALL ways!"

~ *Your Child*

One cannot take the parent or child job without the other filling in the other position! Parents can't be parents without the children, and children can't be children without the parents. You are clearly in this together and clearly here as equals! You both nourish each other with guidance, love, and wisdom—and are both equally responsible for shifting each other to BE and live in your soul-center. That IS why you and your children are here in this physical life—to trust one another!

Keep in mind that the change in the job taking and filling for who the spiritual and who the physical teachers or students are is a constant one, so be on alert Mom and Dad.

Your children are speedsters!

If trouble arises, stop and ask yourself honestly:

"Am I filling the right job right now?"

"Am I studying the right subject right now?"

"Is my child teaching me physically or spiritually right now?"

"Am I dancing a harmonious dance with my child?"

To harmonize, quit the unfitting job that you are holding on for dear life, and with your deepest gratitude, go fill the right and fitting one for right now. No harm done, just a bit of clarity needed and a wonderful adjustment accomplished!

This IS Parenting Through the Eyes of Lollipops!

GRATITUDE, APPRECIATION, RESPECT, AND ACCEPTANCE

"Gratitude, appreciation, respect, and acceptance is something that I learn from witnessing you in how you feel it, practice it, voice it, and show it."

~ *Your Child*

Imagine a bee pollinating everything, and that at some point a plant, flower, or fruit is growing. The bee never considers to stop or re-think its purpose just because whatever it is pollinating

takes time to bloom—instead, the bee knows and trusts in the process and majestically keeps doing what it does best, what makes it the happiest, and what it promised to do when coming into this physical life as a bee.

You are that bee, pollinating everyone and everything - especially your children - with gratitude, appreciation, respect, and acceptance—knowing in your soul that at some point there will be beautiful flowers and fruit to harvest.

So go pollinate, never stop or give up, and never question the outcome—because your trust in this process and majestically doing what you do best, what makes you happiest, and what you promised to do when deciding to be a parent, will grow for you to harvest grateful, appreciative, respectful, and accepting children.

"Appreciation is a conscious gratefulness of my presence, my essence, and my graciousness of being here with you.

Gratitude is a conscious appreciation of my presence, my essence, and my graciousness of being here with you.

Respect is a conscious acceptance of my presence, my essence, and my graciousness of being here with you.

Acceptance is a conscious respect of my presence, my essence, and my graciousness of being here with you."

~ *Your Child*

Gratitude, appreciation, respect, and acceptance start with the parents being grateful, respectful, accepting, and appreciative of their children to simply BE in their life—without any expectations of performance or results. No matter how your children behave, who they choose to be, or how they live, the fact that they chose to come into your life to co-create has to be enough of a reason for you to feel unconditional love for them.

I can't stress enough how much a pure "Thank you!" said from parent to child means to that child—say these healing words often, best without reason, and always with a smile.

From that basic foundation you have the opportunity to add on layer after layer of gratitude, appreciation, respect, and acceptance to make your parenthood experience even richer—like you would paint a color with layers after layers to make the color-experience richer.

Here is how you create those layers:

- Be grateful, appreciative, respectful, and accepting of all the ups and downs, and lefts and rights, that your child is gifting you to experience

- Be grateful, appreciative, respectful, and accepting for all the old unfitting emotional "gunk" your child mirrors you to see, heal, and cleanse yourself from

- Be grateful, appreciative, respectful, and accepting for all of the teaching and studying you get to experience through your children—and with your children

That solid foundation and those rich layers of these noble energies - gratitude, appreciation, respect, and acceptance - will flow over for your child to experience too—remember, everyone is energy and sharing their energy at all times. You are sharing noble-ness here!

With that kind of exhibition, your child will show you gratitude, appreciation, respect, and acceptance freely and willingly—real and pure, straight from your child's heart. A wonderful experience that always feels good; versus the alternative, asking your child to be grateful, appreciative, respectful, and accepting, or pointing out the lack of these behaviors. This will never feel as wonderful as you were hoping it would, because it is not given freely—nor is it truly felt by the child.

Plus, when asking them, you most likely need their gratitude, appreciation, respect, or acceptance to feel better or soothe yourself. No wonder your child will not want to give into that, because your child loves you way too much to give you what needs to be filled by you.

If your child lacks gratitude, appreciation, respect, or acceptance, turn inward and work on your foundation of these noble feelings. Then paint beautiful layers by showing all this noble-ness for yourself and for your children—drenching them in a highly noble energy. See what happens!

If that still won't spark the goodness you were hoping for, know that your children always are doing the best they can right now. So love them for that and don't lose your own noble focus. Keep showering yourself and your children—knowing that, whenever they can, they will catch up and take part in the exchange. Be grateful for that!

Keep in mind that the change in the job taking and filling for who the spiritual and who the physical teachers or students are is a constant one, so be on alert Mom and Dad.

Your children are speedsters!

If trouble arises, stop and ask yourself honestly:

"Am I filling the right job right now?"

"Am I studying the right subject right now?"

"Is my child teaching me physically or spiritually right now?"

"Am I dancing a harmonious dance with my child?"

To harmonize, quit the unfitting job that you are holding on for dear life, and with your deepest gratitude, go fill the right and fitting one for right now. No harm done, just a bit of clarity needed and a wonderful adjustment accomplished!

This IS Parenting Through the Eyes of Lollipops!

PATIENCE

"Imagine me as a hammer, and your patience as a nail. That hammer hits the nail over and over, and again and again, making the nail appear shorter and shorter until there is no more patience to hammer in. That is what I am here to do for you with your patience!"

~ Your Child

Patience is one of those things that your children promised to unleash in you and help you grow when they chose to come into your life.

"Mom, Dad, it is a given for you to become a super-patient person because I am here to test, to try to break, and to fortify your patience by being me! You are so very welcome!"

~ Your Child

Even though you are the nail in this and are getting hit from all sides at times, it does not mean that you have to disappear into the wood until you are so short that you are not visible anymore. On the contrary, your opportunity to connect better, bigger, clearer, and more graciously to your soul being is incredible because that is what patience is after all—you being so sure in your knowing that nothing ever has to be, yet everything is always allowed to be if the time and place is right.

"Watching you being patient teaches me how to be patient, because let's face it, patience is not something that my soul being is calling me to do in my young physical life."

~ Your Child

So hurry and grow your patience muscles by strengthening your self-esteem, by deepening your self-knowing, and by heightening your self-belief—creating pure satisfaction for who you are and how you feel. And, when in dire need, say, think, feel, and have a good giggle with saying something like this:

"I know who I am, and certainly am not going to lose my marbles over my offspring trying to nail me!"

When you are at your wits' end…

Instead of focusing on your children - the hammer that is doing what a hammer is supposed to do - when running out of patience focus on yourself - the nail - by connecting deeper with your soul being, and watch your children stop hammering almost immediately. Because, after all, how fun is it to hammer a nail that does not go in?

Keep in mind that the change in the job taking and filling for who the spiritual and who the physical teachers or students are is a constant one, so be on alert Mom and Dad.

Your children are speedsters!

If trouble arises, stop and ask yourself honestly:

"Am I filling the right job right now?"

"Am I studying the right subject right now?"

"Is my child teaching me physically or spiritually right now?"

"Am I dancing a harmonious dance with my child?"

To harmonize, quit the unfitting job that you are holding on for dear life, and with your deepest gratitude, go fill the right and fitting one for right now. No harm done, just a bit of clarity needed and a wonderful adjustment accomplished!

This IS Parenting Through the Eyes of Lollipops!

YOUR CHILDREN'S HIGHEST POTENTIAL

"When you look through the eyes of your soul being - which is pure positive energy - all you can see me as is pure positive energy too—a soul being."

~ *Your Child*

Seeing, thinking of, and feeling your children as their true soul being means that you see them in their highest potential—sharing your admiration for them, drenching them in well-feeling, and inviting them to shift into the realm of their greatest potential. Thinking so highly of them lets you hold their true space for them to fully BE and live as this physical person they came here to experience!

But there is more…

This gracious way of feeling about your children has the wonderful benefit of you shifting yourself into your soul space of your own highest potential as well. And guess what? That means more goodness to share and spread!

So even when things are iffy with your children on a physical life level, you always have the option - and should take advantage of it - to shift your focus away from feeling, seeing, and thinking of all the trouble that's there—instead, go all energetic and focus on their pure positive energy, their highest potential, and their powerful soul being. Hold yourself and them in that gorgeous space with determination—for them and for yourself.

Once the air clears, you can tippy-toe back into all physical life matters, and don't be surprised if the issue has blown over. Those issues, they do that!

Keep in mind that the change in the job taking and filling for who the spiritual and who the physical teachers or students are is a constant one, so be on alert Mom and Dad.

Your children are speedsters!

If trouble arises, stop and ask yourself honestly:

"Am I filling the right job right now?"

"Am I studying the right subject right now?"

"Is my child teaching me physically or spiritually right now?"

"Am I dancing a harmonious dance with my child?"

To harmonize, quit the unfitting job that you are holding on for dear life, and with your deepest gratitude, go fill the right and fitting one for right now. No harm done, just a bit of clarity needed and a wonderful adjustment accomplished!

This IS Parenting Through the Eyes of Lollipops!

Way to go parents! You ARE my heroes!

~ Jacqueline Pirtle

Made in the USA
Middletown, DE
01 November 2020

23147294R00116